OXFORD IN ASIA HISTORICAL MEMOIRS

General Editor: WILLIAM R. ROFF

SPECIAL GUEST

Abdul Aziz Ishak

SPECIAL GUEST

The Detention in Malaysia of an Ex-Cabinet Minister

ISBN 0 19 580378 8 (Board)
ISBN 0 19 580373 7 (Limp)

ABDUL AZIZ ISHAK

SINGAPORE
OXFORD UNIVERSITY PRESS
LONDON NEW YORK MELBOURNE
1977

Oxford University Press

OXFORD LONDON GLASGOW

NEW YORK TORONTO MELBOURNE WELLINGTON

IBADAN NAIROBI DAR ES SALAAM LUSAKA CAPE TOWN

KUALA LUMPUR SINGAPORE JAKARTA HONG KONG TOKYO

DELHI BOMBAY CALCUTTA MADRAS KARACHI

© *Oxford University Press 1977*

ISBN 0 19 580338 8 (*Boards*)

ISBN 0 19 580361 2 (*Boards*)
ISBN 0 19 580377 9 (*Limp*)

*Printed in Singapore by Dainippon Tien Wah Printing (Pte) Ltd.
Published by Oxford University Press,
41, Jalan Pemimpin, Singapore 20*

To
My One and Only Wife
Wan Shamsiah

*I speak truth, not so much as I would,
but as much as I dare; and I dare a little
more as I grow older.*

MONTAIGNE, *Essays III*

CONTENTS

CONTENTS
PART III

FOREWORD

THIS is the story of the detention in Malaysia of a public figure, a man who was for seven-and-a-half years a Minister in the Alliance Cabinet, from 1955 until 1963, when he resigned over differences in policy. That former Minister is myself. This is my story, and I vouch for its truth. My reasons for publishing *Special Guest* are both public and private, but both have the same aim—to exonerate my name. The public reason is simply that I feel very deeply that the people of Malaysia, my own country, should know what happened to a man they trusted, and whom they have been led mistakenly to believe is not worthy of their trust.

In reading this book, it should be remembered that Indonesia had at the time of these events turned from the passive policy of confrontation against Malaysia to a state of undeclared war by actual invasion of our shores in 1964. Malaysia was, of course, under a State of Emergency.

I was arrested under the Internal Security Act in January 1965, accused of being a traitor to my country in that I had actively collaborated with Indonesia to assist their energy forces.

I was released—if one can use that word to apply in my case—under restriction as to my freedom of movement, freedom of political or union activities, and banned from leaving my own country. The first term of restriction lasted one year but it was renewed by Orders three times thereafter—my final unconditional release not taking place until March 1971. Thus, I was a man under duress, either in confinement or restricted, for a period of seven years.

The private reason for my authorship of this story of detention is my belief in that basic principle of law, that 'not only must justice be done, but it must be seen to be done'. In my case this has not happened. True, my arrest and my release were well publicized by the authorities. These covered a period of one year. From 1966 to 1971, the authorities kept quiet about all action taken against me subsequent to my actual release from one year in confinement. It seems they preferred that I should be regarded as a forgotten man. In doing so, my name is still under a cloud.

Well, I am no longer prepared to be an inhabitant of Limbo, and so I have written this book. It is my hope that my countrymen will learn from my experiences, because an injustice to one is an injustice to all. Only truth can be true. If we allow ourselves to become afraid of truth then the time will come when we will bitterly regret our indifference.

I have tried to the best of my ability to be as fair as I can to all concerned. I have deliberately omitted, except in two instances, all names relating to the authorities in the Special Branch or their juniors or their agents, so that they will not be identifiable by the general public. I made a promise during my detention that I would not allow any of my activities to embarrass the Government, of which I was formerly a Minister. I kept that promise. In this book, I have written in the same spirit. If considered critical, then it will be rather of procedures, methods and decisions—not policy. I trust, therefore, that the authorities may extend to me the same right to criticize as they reserve for themselves. Is not that a basis of democracy?

In presenting this book to the world at large, I wish especially to express my gratitude to an old friend, Frank Sullivan, for the invaluable help he has so readily given me to bring my story into the open.

Kuala Lumpur,   ABDUL AZIZ ISHAK
1976

PROLOGUE

Some people act and think as though they had not been born mortals as others were, but had been carefully lowered from heaven.

SEAN O'CASEY

I. THE BIRTH OF MALAY NATIONALISM

My first meeting with Tunku Abdul Rahman Putra was in Penang in 1936. Mr. M. Saravanamuthu, then Editor of a North Malayan daily, *The Straits Echo*, was the friend who introduced us at a cabaret. Sara, as he was popularly known, later became Ambassador for Ceylon to Indonesia.

I was then twenty-two years old, a probationer Fisheries Officer covering North Malaya, and I had met Sara some months earlier, strangely enough also at the same cabaret. I remember this because for the first time in my life I was mentioned in a newspaper, not only in the news items but also in a subsidiary editorial. A glut of fish, known as *shad* or herring, had invaded the northern shores of the Peninsula, and as a result hundreds of tons of fish rotted on landing and could find no market. The editorial made it seem as if I was responsible. I protested to Sara against this unfair charge, and after explaining the true situation we became good friends.

In the middle of 1951, fifteen years later, I met the Tunku again, though he did not remember me. This was after he was elected president of the United Malays National Organisation, replacing Datuk Onn bin Jaafar, the first National President. Ever since then our paths have crossed and recrossed under all manner of circumstances.

UMNO, the first truly organized Malay political party, emerged as a result of the Malayan Union proposals in August 1945, after the war in South-East Asia was over.

During the three-and-a-half years of the occupation of Malaya by Japanese military forces, the political consciousness of the people of Malaya was encouraged by the Japanese and the Malays especially responded readily. Malay nationalism, which, during the years of British colonial rule was cleverly suppressed, had its

secretive beginning in 1938 when the Kesatuan Melayu Muda
was organized under Ibrahim bin Haji Yaakob, Onan bin Haji
Siraj, and Mustapha Haji Hussein, to mention only a few. The
membership of K.M.M., as it was known in brief, comprised
young Malay intellectuals. I was just an ordinary member, but
years later when a delegation of Alliance Ministers visited Jakarta,
Ibrahim Yaakob informed the Tunku that he was proud that
Kesatuan Melayu Muda was represented in the Tunku 'Cabinet'
of 1946 in the person of myself.

When the Japanese Armed Forces surrendered and the British
Government returned to Malaya, the people were shocked when
the Malayan Union Plan was announced simultaneously in London and in Singapore on 10 October 1945. This plan, among
other changes, wanted to transform the status of Malaya from a
pre-war British protectorate to that of a colony. The nine Malay
States, together with Penang and Malacca, the last two hitherto
British colonies, were all to become politically and administratively
one, and to be headed by a British Governor with almost unlimited
powers to rule the country. The Malay Rulers or Sultans were
relegated to the position of *Imam* or *Kathi,* functioning only in
the fields of Islamic religion and Malay customs.

The Secretary of State for the Colonies, in making this announcement, timed it so well that two days later, i.e. one day after
the announcement appeared in the local press, Sir Harold Mac-
Michael, an experienced British Colonial Service Officer, was
commissioned to obtain the signatures of Malay Rulers agreeing
to the Malayan Union, by any manner possible. Sir Harold did
not at the outset use democratic methods in achieving his objective.
The Rulers were coaxed into signing, without the advice of their
Councils of Advisers. The result was that the Malay press, with
the *Utusan Melayu* in Singapore, the *Majlis* in Kuala Lumpur and
the *Warta Negara* in Penang, mounted separate attacks, but were
united in condemning the Malayan Union editorially. They also
published an unending stream of letters of protest from readers
throughout the country.

This resulted in eight Malay Associations, hitherto non-political
in nature, forming the Malay League of Johore and in January
1946 the Peninsular Malay Movement, also of Johore, came into

being under the leadership of Datuk Onn bin Jaafar.

At the suggestion of the Malay Press a meeting of all Malay organizations throughout the country was held on 1 March 1946. This was the first Malay political congress, with forty-one bodies represented. The meeting was unanimous in agreeing to establish a Pan-Malay Congress, which was later formed. From then on these Malay parties began to unite and consolidate.

The Congress not only protested against the Malayan Union, but went one step further by asking Whitehall to agree to give freedom to Malaya as a matter of principle, but met with no response.

What perhaps changed the mind of the Government was the pressure after the visit of two British Members of Parliament on a fact-finding mission to Malaya to assess the degree of opposition to the Malayan Union. L. Gammans, and David Rees-Williams, later Lord Ogmore, both former residents of Malaya before the war, met Datuk Onn and others, including myself, in Singapore before crossing over to meet other leaders on the mainland.

It could be said that the Malayan Union was God's plan as a stepping stone to the formation of UMNO and later to Independence or *Merdeka* for the country. UMNO, however, was considered a middle-of-the-road party from the very beginning. Opposed to it even during the formation of the Congress was the left-wing Malay Nationalist Party which was formed earlier, with its youth organization known as Angkatan Pemuda Insaf. Its leader was Ahmad Boestamam, who was detained by the British just before the Japanese came to Malaya, and later suffered detention three more times under the Internal Security Act.

The Malayan Union was later abolished and replaced by a new Constitution of the Federation of Malaya in 1948. It came into being on 21 January of that year. This new Constitution returned sovereignty to the Malay Rulers. The British Government, however, was responsible for defence and external affairs of the Federation of Malaya. But the left-wing groups were not entirely happy about the change. However, it was a step forward for the Malays towards *Merdeka*.

Datuk Onn, the President of UMNO, was truly the hero of the Malays in the struggle to abolish the Malayan Union. But by 1948 Malay leaders began to assess the future of Malay politics and how UMNO should plan its objectives. Datuk Onn can be said to have been ahead of his time in wanting to open UMNO to the other communities. His forward thinking was not well received at subsequent meetings of the UMNO general assemblies. He also envisaged the relaxation of the citizenship law of the Federation of Malaya Agreement to make it less difficult for other races to become citizens. As a result of his proposal he resigned twice, once in 1950, which he later withdrew after much persuasion from the floor, but finally resigned at the next UMNO General Assembly on 27 August 1951. He left, together with some UMNO leaders, to form a new party known as the Independence of Malaya Party in September the same year. It is important to record that when UMNO was formed the British Government did not feel that its own leadership would be in danger from rapid progress to *Merdeka* or Independence. The British, however, rather feared a situation, as in Indonesia, when the demand for independence of that country snowballed within a short space of time. This could be reflected in the policy whereby the Special Branch of the police kept a very close surveillance on extremist leaders in UMNO, especially the younger groups. It was unheard of for Malay leaders to utter openly the slogan *Merdeka* at this time. But with the formation of the Independence of Malaya Party, the much-feared word became a reality and was made legal with a stroke of the pen. One of the Independence of Malaya Party's slogans was the attainment of *Merdeka* within ten years. Like many others, I left UMNO to join the Independence of Malaya Party for this very reason. I was elected to the National Executive Council of the new party and later became vice-chairman of the Kuala Lumpur branch, while Datuk Onn himself became chairman.

Soon after the war was over, another youth organization, Gerakan Angkatan Melayu Malaya, or GERAM, was formed. I was its President, with Thaharuddin Ahmad, a former head of *Antara*, an Indonesian news agency representative in Malaya, as my deputy. A. Samad Ismail, then a member of the editorial staff of the *Utusan Melayu*, acted as Secretary. The formation of GERAM was motivated by the apparent reason that while UMNO was too slow-going, MNP was too much geared to the tempo of the Indonesian Independence demand. GERAM was to be the half-way party. But apart from making a few statements against the Federation of Malaya Agreement and sending our representatives to attend youth conferences in India nothing much was achieved. When I moved to Kuala Lumpur in 1948, the party, after being refused registration, died a natural death.

In 1948 the *Utusan Melayu*, with its head office in Singapore, appointed me as its Malayan representative based in Kuala Lumpur. In those days all important national dailies, including the English language dailies, functioned from Singapore. As I said earlier, my association with the Tunku came about only after he took over UMNO from Datuk Onn. At the beginning it was purely a relationship of a newspaperman and a party leader. However, in this capacity and also that of the vice-president of the Press Club of Malaya, I had on a few occasions played host to the Tunku and Datuk Abdul Razak bin Hussein, his deputy. Datuk Onn too on several occasions was a guest of the Press Club. Apart from playing the role of a newspaper reporter in February 1951 I was also nominated to the Federal Legislative Council. The Tunku, however, did not join the Council until August that year, by virtue of being head of UMNO.

With the formation of the Independence of Malaya Party, UMNO joined forces with the Malayan Chinese Association, or M.C.A., to form the vanguard of the Alliance. When the Government announced the country's first general elections for the Kuala Lumpur Municipality, I was a candidate for one of the Malay-dominated wards in the Kampung Bahru area. The people of Kuala Lumpur were for the first time experiencing election fever. Both parties mounted a campaign with the thoroughness and intensity reported to be normal in the United Kingdom. At least it was a copybook type of campaign. Leaders and workers of the Independence of Malaya Party were briefed by Datuk Onn himself, armed with several handbooks on elections from the Labour and Conservative Parties of England. However, the net result was that, after the three successful UMNO candidates in the elections, J ran fourth, only 92 votes behind the last successful candidate. A few months later I resigned my membership of the Independence of Malaya Party because of personal differences with Datuk

Onn. In an article in the *Mastika*, a monthly journal of the Utusan Melayu Press, I mentioned that neither Datuk Onn nor Tunku Abdul Rahman as political leaders in the country would be able to achieve the country's independence for the *ra'ayat*, because both of them had an aristocratic background.

On resigning from the Independence of Malaya Party I was determined to remain unattached to any political party, so that I could carry on my newspaper work without being a partisan. At this time I was also a member of the Editorial Board and contributed editorials on Malayan matters. I met the Tunku on a few occasions after leaving the Independence of Malaya Party and later our paths seemed to drift together, and when he was in Kuala Lumpur which was at least once a week to attend the Federal Executive Council, he would look for me to have a chat. In Kuala Lumpur at that time he had few friends with whom he could talk and discuss matters intelligently. He found a good listener in me. Our friendship became close. About this time I did some liaison work for him with the Press. In the middle of 1952 when he gave his first press conference to foreign journalists in Singapore, I was there with him. Later in the year when I was in hospital in Kuala Lumpur for the removal of an appendix, he was a frequent visitor.

The sponsors of the proposed World Federation Government invited other well-known personalities from Malaya to the conference through me personally. This was the splinter body of the World Pacifists Meeting held in Santeneketan in India, which I attended in 1949. The Tunku accepted the invitation to attend the conference which took us on a round trip of more than a month by sea on board a British India boat. In Japan we spent eleven days at the conference at Hiroshima and visited many places, including Tokyo, Kobe, Atami and Nara. Among those who attended the conference were Lord Boyd-Orr, the first Director-General of the United Nations Agency Food and Agricultural Organisation immediately after the war, and Mr. Justice Paul who successfully defended the Indian National Army Officers from Malaya as war criminals, before he was elevated to the Indian bench, to name only two.

On our way to Japan I mentioned to the Tunku that I had

completed my nomination papers for the coming election of the Kuala Lumpur Municipality as an Independent Candidate and that my sponsors would present it to the Returning Officer on the appointed date. The Tunku without hesitation sent a cable to Kuala Lumpur UMNO Headquarters asking them not to oppose my application. Perhaps the cable did not arrive in time, because the Alliance legal adviser made an objection to a typographical error found on my nomination paper.

It was not until April 1953 that I rejoined UMNO. The circumstances leading to this were rather unusual. One day when the Tunku was still living in Johore Bahru, where UMNO Headquarters was, I went to see him on my way home from Singapore after attending a Board of Directors meeting of the Utusan Melayu Press. After the usual small talk he came down and tied an UMNO car badge to the grill of my car and said, 'This is a present from me. Now, Aziz, get yourself registered as a member.' I went home in deep thought all the way to Kuala Lumpur. In Kuala Lumpur I became a member of UMNO for the second time.

In June 1953 I was in England for the Coronation of Queen Elizabeth the Second and on my return the Tunku appointed me to the Alliance Round Table Conference, established while I was away. Its purpose was to make preparations in a closed discussion to demand an early date for general elections for the country. In the latter part of the year I was also nominated a candidate of the Alliance to contest the Kuala Lumpur Municipal election for Bungsar Ward which was predominantly an Indian area. My visit to England to cover the coronation was a turning point in my political career, when the High Commissioner, Sir Gerald Templer, scolded me for my coverage of the Coronation Ceremony and other news items I filed from England for the *Utusan Melayu*. The Malayan press became a readers' forum for some months afterwards and I became a minor hero among the people, particularly among UMNO members.

At the Bungsar Ward election, despite efforts by the pro-Government elements to discredit me, I won the seat. In the latter part of 1954, I obtained leave for one month from the *Utusan Melayu* to accompany the Tunku on an intensive campaign for the State elections of Kelantan and Trengganu. Both the Tunku's wife and mine formed part of the team. During this period as many as five rallies were held each day at which both the Tunku and I spoke to audiences of never less than two thousand and as many as ten thousand each time. When the Federal Legislative Council met on our return from the East Coast, I took the opportunity to give a report of the electioneering campaign, mentioning the part played by British District Officers in dissuading the people from attending the rallies. This was also an exciting period in the Legislative Council, being the eve of the general election when members of Party Negara, the successor to the Independence of Malaya Party, crossed swords with those of the Alliance, often with much heat and rancour.

The year of the general election was a busy one for me. Apart from being chairman of the Selangor Alliance I was also given the function of a mediator when problems in the Alliance Headquarters in Negeri Sembilan became difficult to resolve. The Negeri Sembilan State Alliance at that time was lacking a firm leader, as had been seen during the Alliance boycott of all Councils of Government, on the issue of the number of elected as opposed to nominated seats in the future Federal Council. During the boycott, I was chairman of the Selangor State Alliance Committee, but since the Alliance in Negeri Sembilan was a little disorganized I was asked by the Tunku to look after Negeri Sembilan as well. In Selangor two State Assemblymen would not co-operate and refused to resign their seats. One was a senior forest officer and the other a member of the Selangor Royal House. It was my unpleasant function to have to expel them from the membership of UMNO.

It was also my task to organize reprisals against the members of the Legislative Council irrespective of whether they belonged to the Alliance or not, as long as they were Malays. Two of them came to Kuala Lumpur to a meeting of the Council. One was later to become Speaker of the Dewan Ra'ayat or House of Representatives (Lower House), the other was a former Trade Union leader. UMNO youth leaders wanted to beat them up but I objected to any kind of violence. The next morning, however, when the delinquents, who were staying at an hotel in Batu Road in Kuala Lumpur, were leaving for the Council meeting they found the upholstery of their cars smeared with unpleasant-smelling matter! Nevertheless they arrived at the meeting—but in a taxi. I was later informed by an UMNO youth leader that they had to engage special car cleaners to have the upholstery regain its normal condition and, of course, smell. The Tunku, when informed of this incident, showed neither approval nor objection.

Three months before the election, around May 1955, the Alliance leaders met every evening to prepare its manifesto. Each one of us was asked to prepare a draft paper on various subjects for the manifestoes, mine was on Information and Publicity. The subject of Malay becoming the national official language and that it should be implemented within ten years was also included in our manifesto. This was the bone of contention between Tunku Abdul Rahman and the people and it was ultimately the last straw that broke the back of Malaya and Malaysia's first Prime Minister. The manifesto as a whole was generally agreed by all to contain brave and high-sounding intentions to make great changes from the Colonial type of Government policy to that of an independent and sovereign country. On the subjects of agriculture, economics, education, finance and the Emergency, etc. we knew what we wanted, the very best for the people and the country, obtained in the best way. The promises contained in the manifesto were explained in detail by the party leaders and candidates. That the people accepted the programme of the Alliance was clear when we secured fifty-one out of fifty-two seats. The other seat went to the Pan-Malayan Islamic Party. Datuk Onn, leading the Party Negara himself, was defeated, together with all his party candidates.

An incident where hooliganism first occurred happened in my own constituency. The Party Negara was backed by the British and had all the Government officers and the administrators behind it. An Alliance information booth near a polling station was wrecked completely by a gang of Party Negara hooligans, while thirty yards away stood a Deputy Superintendent of Police, a Malayan of Indian descent. When this incident took place I was a few hundred yards away, but rushed back when told of it. When I confronted the police officer, he coolly told me that at that time he was not looking in the direction of my demolished information booth. Ten years later the same officer was promoted to Superintendent, while officers much junior to him had two or three promotions above him.

During this first general election other parties in the Alliance, particularly M.C.A., were given seats in Malay-dominated areas, or in areas where Alliance supporters were strong. This meant that UMNO candidates had to contest in areas where support was doubtful. But being the senior member of the Alliance we had to make this sacrifice. For my part as leader of the Selangor Alliance I chose the most indifferent constituency and was pitted against a strong man of Party Negara. I won, but not by a substantial majority.

A week later when the first Alliance Ministers list in the Cabinet was announced I was appointed Minister for Agriculture and placed sixth on the list of seniority. Frankly, I was disappointed as I thought I would be placed a little higher because of my seniority in the Legislative Council since 1951, as a nominated member. I mentioned this to the Tunku and he was quite prepared to let me go up a step over the head of the next person above me, but I declined. It could have been done earlier without embarrassment to anyone.

However, when other members of UMNO came to live in Kuala Lumpur after the formation of the Alliance Cabinet, the beginning of a rift was already on the horizon.

It was inevitable that with other top members of the Alliance living in Kuala Lumpur, there would be keen competition for the Tunku's favours. I being what I am, a blunt person, as some people have labelled me, did not go out of my way to preserve my personal standing with him. On the other hand, while I did not change, a few changes began to appear in the Tunku, who had begun to feel the sense of growing power and position, and with new advisers around him the change was swift. In short, I began within six months of the election to be already out of favour. One of the first disagreements was the wearing of the uniform for Cabinet Ministers, which I objected to rather strongly, and for the first few occasions I refrained from attending official functions where uniforms had to be worn. After this I began to sense a mild feeling of hostility towards me from the Tunku and

Tun Razak. I was left out of the more important delegations going overseas. Only at my insistence was I included in the delegation to Bangkok and Jakarta led by the Tunku as Chief Minister. Those were the only two missions to the neighbouring countries in which I was included. At the end of 1956 I was, however, not disappointed, bitter or angry about not being a member of the Merdeka mission to London.

It is not my intention in this book to write a detailed autobiography, only the story leading to the break-up with my colleagues in the Alliance Cabinet, with the Tunku as a leading figure.

From the outset in August 1955, I took to the country, travelling with heads of departments in my Ministry to familiarize myself with what was going on in the field, and at the same time to meet State Officers of the various departments of Agriculture, Forestry, Fisheries, Drainage and Irrigation and the Resettlement of Special Constables. The last-named department dealt with demobilized Special Constables as the Emergency situation improved. Later, when the Department of Co-operative Development came under my Portfolio I tried to pick up as quickly as possible problems which required reassessment and the restructuring of policy after the colonial system.

In fact, most of my time was spent in the rural areas throughout the length and breadth of Malaya, among farmers, fishermen and others connected with rural and community developments. My idea was to tackle the problems on the spot and to make as few mistakes as possible in the implementation of the Ministry's new policy that I was about to formulate. When I visited Thailand with the official delegation with Tunku Abdul Rahman in December 1955, I stayed on to study the rural projects of that country.

Again, when I visited Indonesia with the Cabinet delegation later in the year, I studied as much as possible how Indonesia tackled its rural programme. In 1956 when I headed a delegation composed of officials from the British colonies at the regional conference of the Food and Agriculture Organisation of the United Nations for Asia and the Far East at Bandung, I was elected deputy chairman of the conference. The late Sir Donald MacGillivray, the last British High Commissioner in Malaya before Independence, at an Executive Council meeting jokingly said: 'This is perhaps a paradox where the person who most hated the British Empire had to lead a British Colonial delegation at an international conference.' After the conference was over I took the opportunity to make a tour of development projects in Indonesia and stayed on a little longer than the others. Sir Robert Scott, the then British Commissioner-General for South-East Asia, reported in a communique through Sir Donald MacGillivray how I acquitted myself during the time I was in Indonesia. It was rather a flattering report about my work as assessed by leaders of delegations at the conference.

Subsequently, in July 1957, officials of my Ministry and I spent three weeks at the invitation of the Indian Government studying community development in Southern India and the surrounding areas of Bombay, and lastly in New Delhi, where I attended the Independence Day celebration. Pandit Nehru in a conversation asked me, 'Why is it that my old friend Tunku Abdul Rahman, who was very kind to me when I visited Kedah after the war, did not think of coming to India but rather preferred to be close to the Australians and New Zealanders?' He asked me to convey his respects to the Tunku and invited him to India. I knew Pandit Nehru previously, when I spent six weeks in India for the World Pacifists Meeting at Santeneketan and Sevagram. The former was the home of the well-known Indian poet Rabindranath Tagore, the latter was the home of Mahatma Gandhi.

A few months later arrangements were made for me to visit Japan as the guest of the Japanese Government for one week. In Japan, the Deputy Ministers of Agriculture—there were several of them—held a series of conferences with me and my Malayan advisers. A tour of agricultural research stations especially for padi was undertaken, also of fishing ports and villages. Japan at that time was acclaimed the leading country in Asia in respect of research in padi growing and her rice yield per acre was the highest in the world, and perhaps still is.

When the official visit was over we stayed on for another week inspecting factories, including a can-making plant, to compare the method and technique with a similar British-owned plant in Singapore. The visit to Japan was indeed rewarding. The then

Japanese Prime Minister, Mr. Nobusuke Kishi, personally directed his Ministers to accede to whatever requests we made for assistance. Finally, before we left for home, the first joint venture in fisheries undertaken with Japan was worked out. A tuna fishing enterprise operating in the Indian Ocean, based in Penang with the co-operatives having a 25% interest, was established eighteen months later, together with local capital divided 51% for Malaya and Japan 49%.

Within six months after our return, teams of Japanese rice experts were invited and came to our research stations to advise on rice-planting techniques, plant breeding, irrigation control, pest control, etc. Expatriate officers in the Ministry, however, threatened to resign in a body before the Japanese experts arrived, if they did come. It was indeed a difficult decision for me to make in view of the Tunku's policy of wanting to retain them for five years after Merdeka. Our country today owes a great debt to these experts in various fields of research rice planting, and who were mainly responsible for the increased yield from our *sawahs* today.

In particular they have helped in the pioneering work of building up padi research capacity, especially in the area of rice variety improvement with the release of high-yielding, good-quality, short-term varieties to sustain and expand rice double cropping. They have also helped in the development of rice-plant water requirement that helped to provide the basis for the planning of the largest irrigation area for padi double-cropping, known as the Great Muda Project in Kedah.

When my colleagues, Tunku Abdul Rahman and the other members of the Cabinet, were sworn in in August 1955, all the ideals of our election platform thrashed out by all the manifestoes of the Alliance Round Table in late 1954 and early 1955 seemed to be workable and possible to implement without much difficulty. In fact, the Alliance Ministers in August 1955 did not yet form a Cabinet in the true sense of the word. We were merely members of the Federal Executive Council with the British High Commissioner as Chairman, the Tunku as Chief Minister next in rank to him, the Chief Secretary ranking after the Chief Minister with the Financial Secretary, the Secretary for Defence, the Secretary for Economic

Affairs, all British colonial officials in order of seniority, then came the Alliance Ministers.

There was a general feeling of euphoria among us and there was not a murmur of protest by the M.C.A. about education, nor from the Malayan Indian Congress about labour problems or Malay as the official language nor from UMNO about business opportunities for the Malays and economic exploitation by the others.

Looking back, I remember telling T.H. Tan, the Secretary-General of the Alliance, at one of the sessions of the Manifesto Committee that the Chinese businessmen in the kampungs should not exploit the Malays anymore. 'This should be the spirit of the Alliance,' I added. T.H. Tan roared with laughter, so did Ong Yoke Lin, a senior M.C.A. member. But the Tunku only smiled and H.S. Lee remained impassive. T.H. Tan finally said that when the election was over we all could recall Aziz's remarks and laugh at them. History has since shown that it was no joking matter.

So when the Manifesto of the Alliance was ready we were all very proud of it. We felt that our Government of the future would be the best in the world. All the Ministers would be dedicated, working solely for the benefit of the masses, the poor would no longer be exploited, we would remove once and forever our dependence on colonial policy and its influence. They were all very sincere, genuine and determined intentions. So it felt to all of us then. What turned out was quite different.

Except for Tunku Abdul Rahman, who became a Member of the Executive Council in his capacity as President of UMNO and the Alliance in 1953, and Dr. Ismail, who held a Government portfolio as a trainee member of self-governing Malaya, also Col. H.S. Lee in 1954, the rest had no experience of how to run a Government. The training of the Tunku, Dr. Ismail and Col. Lee was of course useful in the British way of running a semi-colonial type of Government but not in the governing of an independent, socialist-tinted form which the Manifesto of the Alliance Party claimed to have as its policy.

The Tunku on many occasions jokingly branded me as the only member of his Government who was a socialist. But, however,

since the British Conservative Government at that time were also
carrying out a policy lifted or borrowed from the Labour Party
of England, so the outline of our Alliance Manifesto seemed
proper.

To think of it now, it seems like a dream on the horizon with
little hope of reaching it. Why do I say this? Because Tunku
Abdul Rahman never tried to go beyond what was drafted in
the Manifesto. In fact the Manifesto was completely forgotten
and never had a chance to be used after we won the first general
election in July 1955. He was so busy preparing for the next step
towards Independence (*Merdeka*), that most of the policy-making
was left to the British colonial officials in Finance, Commerce
and Industry, Defence, etc. Whenever he was reminded of our
Manifesto, he said it could wait until after Independence was
achieved.

After having failed several times to draw his attention to the
promises we had made to the electorate, I concentrated on my
portfolio of Agriculture.

The round of social parties and protocol took quite a lot of
Tunku's time, including his insistence on designing a Minister's
uniform to resemble that of British Colonial Governors, complete
with gold-embroidered shoulder badge and a rich collar decoration
with something like an oak leaf on it. The headgear had red and
white plumes on a cocked-hat with a white sharkskin jacket or
tunic with dark slacks. There were of course no medals or awards
worn as yet. But a few years later medals and decorations sometimes could not find enough space on some of the Ministers'
jackets where decorations were normally worn.

In fact the Manifesto was quite forgotten until the election in
1959. The policy on this occasion was to vote for the Tunku
personally, not minding if earlier promises were not kept, as we
had already achieved Merdeka. It had been a well-known habit
of the Tunku after Independence was declared to claim that there
was not even a single drop of blood shed. Also, that he was the
happiest Prime Minister in the world. During all this time however
there was a minimum of murmuring and rumblings of complaint
which of course the Tunku ignored. Suddenly 13 May 1969 exploded and brought a considerable amount of bloodshed in its

train. This spelled his fall from grace. A year later he retired as
the first Prime Minister of Malaysia.

II. MINISTER OF AGRICULTURE BEFORE MERDEKA

SINCE we were boys, my brother, Yusof, and I had been of similar nature. A nature often inclined to be openly critical of things we found not quite right. This trait of outspokenness often got us into trouble. But above all we tried in every way to uphold truth and very often suffered for it.

When I joined the *Utusan Melayu*, Yusof was Editor, as he had been all the time, and concurrently the Managing Director, and I was later to become a member of the editorial board and also a director of the company. On the whole, in respect of freedom of the Press, my late brother agreed with me that we had much more freedom in the editorial column in the days before Merdeka. Before Merdeka, *Utusan Melayu* not only co-operated with the Alliance by projecting its policy but also spearheaded the attack on British exploitation of the country and the people, especially Malays. But on achieving Merdeka the Alliance leaders were intolerant of fair comments and criticism by the *Utusan Melayu* and later by the Press generally. Measured by the standard of fair criticism without fear or favour the British Colonial Government based on centuries of democracy had no comparison. Our journalists now are sad examples of the new breed common in most emerging countries, where true freedom of the Press is now a thing of the past.

Yusof, before the *Utusan Melayu* moved from Singapore to Kuala Lumpur, felt that the golden opportunity had come for the paper to work for the alleviation of the people and the country in the only democratic way he knew, when he became a newspaperman both during the British Colonial period and also during the Japanese Occupation of our country for three-and-a-half years. The *Utusan Melayu* began to be out of favour with Tunku Abdul Rahman and other UMNO leaders not long after

Malaya achieved Merdeka. And thereafter the tempo and volume of impatience with comments and criticisms of the *Utusan Melayu* increased in proportion to the Alliance gaining power and strength in the country and its reputation in the world at large.

Before my brother went to Singapore I suggested that Tunku Abdul Rahman should bestow on him a suitable honour for his work in the *Utusan Melayu*. This was for the period soon after the return of the British following the surrender of the Japanese forces in 1945, and also when he spearheaded the anti-Malayan Union mass media and later directed the fight for Merdeka. The Tunku suggested giving him the J.M.N. (*Johan Mangku Negara*). When I told my brother about it, I had the impression that he expected something better, but I managed to persuade him to accept it.

But when it came to the knowledge of Tun Abdul Razak, he objected even to this. I did my best to impress on both the Tunku and Razak the great contribution that Yusof had made to the country. With shame I had to tell my brother of Razak's attitude.

However, when Singapore was in Malaysia, Yusof became a Tun, a far cry from a mere J.M.N., and after my release from detention I stayed with him at the Istana in Singapore. He related to me an incident which again perhaps showed God's handiwork in compensation for all the humiliation Yusof had earlier received from the Tunku and some of the Rulers. At a Ruler's garden party, when all of them were seated, the Yang di-Pertuan Agung was the central figure, with the others placed in accordance with protocol and Yusof as the Yang di-Pertuan Negara of Singapore placed the lowest in seniority. Along the line of august personages he was seated last on the extreme left. The Governors of Penang and Malacca had precedence over him. The Istana Negara organizers felt that this was a suitable occasion to show off a dancing camel presented to the Yang di-Pertuan Agung by the then President of Pakistan, General Ayub Khan, after the King's visit to that country.

Days before the great occasion the dancing camel, suitably dressed with glittering accoutrements, including many little bells, went through several rehearsals. Dummies of the Rulers and the Governors were used during the rehearsals and the dancing camel would, according to plan, make an obeisance to the central figure of the King. All was well. On the great day, however, when a feeling of general merriment was felt after the Conference of Rulers was over, the august gathering was to see the great performance of the dancing camel. The camel trainer in appropriate ceremonial attire led it down the line of Rulers and Governors who were very dignified in their regal dress, their faces denoting expectant pleasure. The camel passed along the line and for a moment hesitated in front of the King but did not stop. Breathing stopped. The air of merriment turned to horror. The camel had stopped in front of the Yang di-Pertuan Negara of Singapore to make its obeisance. My brother was, however, quick in trying to soften the blow by making a suitable joke. He remarked that it was a great mistake for this to have happened (after the camel had been quickly led away). 'The poor camel,' he said, 'made a mistake simply because it was homesick. In making the salute to me he mistook me for General Ayub. The shape of my nose is not unlike General Ayub's.'

Even before the headquarters of the *Utusan Melayu* moved to Kuala Lumpur there had already been a few mild brushes between my successor in Kuala Lumpur and the Alliance leaders, when I had tried to act as mediator. On one occasion my brother had to fly to Kuala Lumpur and a dinner was arranged, with the Tunku as host at the Residency. Yusof was accompanied by Mr. Lee Kuan Yew, at that time the legal adviser to the Utusan Melayu Press. The dinner was for four of us, I was the fourth. As was usual with the Tunku, what with good food and drink he was in an expansive and generous mood to compromise with Yusof. And after an agreement was reached about the ground rules to be observed *vis-à-vis* the Utusan Melayu and the Government, it ended quite happily for both parties.

But unfortunately amidst good-byes, Yusof's parting shot did not please either the Tunku or Lee Kuan Yew. Yusof said, 'Now let us see who will keep his part of the bargain.' Eventually the Tunku took over the *Utusan Melayu*, buying up the majority shares from members of our family when Yusof could not bear any further embarrassment and threats.

Finally, when Yusof had sold out his interest in *Utusan Melayu*, Lee Kuan Yew invited Yusof to go back to Singapore, after he had been in Kuala Lumpur for two years, since 1958. First he was appointed Chairman of the Singapore Public Service Commission and later Yang di-Pertuan Negara. And on Singapore's secession from Malaysia in 1965, he became the first President of the Republic.

III. THE BEGINNING OF A RIFT

In the interval between the general election of 1955 and Merdeka in 1957, several Cabinet committees were set up. Each one consisted of about half Alliance Ministers and half from the ranks of British officials in the Cabinet, with the Tunku as Chairman. The Committee on Malayanization was ranked quite high in priority and urgency because we were to determine the number of British expatriate officers to be retained after Merdeka, according to their category of service. I was a member of this Committee and also sat on several others.

It was obvious that most British officers would opt to stay on after Merdeka in 1957. They had their own reasons for wanting to remain in the country. Very often, however, they claimed that it would be in Malaya's interest for them to continue to serve. For my part I had my own reasons for not wanting to retain them longer than necessary as they would be inclined to consider their services indispensable. In this situation, there would be every likelihood of their watering down important changes of policy required for a newly-independent country. Speaking personally as Minister of Agriculture, after only a few weeks in the saddle, I discovered that many of these officers wanted to carry out a policy of perpetuating the *status quo* of the Colonial Government. This was perhaps inevitable since vast British economic interests in agriculture and mining had to be protected and maintained.

For my part I always held the belief that given the opportunity a Malayan qualified officer is no inferior to an expatriate. But my conviction was not shared by some of my colleagues.

The Tunku, the Chairman, was at the outset briefed not to be hasty in dispensing with the services of the expatriates. Hence he was always a picture of caution and consideration. On the other hand I was the leader of a small pressure group on the Committee for rapid Malayanization.

Also, I felt that it would be grossly unfair to the many qualified local officers who would have to wait for some years yet before they were able to show their worth in leadership and responsibility.

Finally, however, the Tunku, as always, had his own way, riding roughshod over all our objections and decided to retain expatriate British officers of the administrative cadre for three to five years, semi-technical officers for not less than five years and technical officers, such as engineers, up to ten years after Merdeka. There was, of course, much disappointment among qualified local officers in the technical and semi-technical services as the result of the Tunku's decision. But the expatriate officers, I was later informed, celebrated the happy event in Kuala Lumpur, toasting the Tunku for his wisdom.

The following account will reflect the attitude of an expatriate officer in my Ministry a few weeks after my appointment. This incident took place at Kuantan when the entire 'Cabinet' was invited for the transfer of the State Capital of Pahang from Kuala Lipis to Kuantan. I directed my Secretary to inform the State Agriculture Officer, an expatriate, to meet me at 5 p.m. the day I arrived at the government Rest House where I was staying. The officer was nowhere to be seen. That evening, however, there was an open-air feast in the grounds of the Government Offices and suddenly I was approached by a European in evening dress, introducing himself as the State Agriculture Officer in a casual manner, offering his hand. I looked at him down and up not taking the offered hand and perhaps in a chilling voice asked him, 'Where were you at 5 p.m. this afternoon?' He muttered something quite inaudible. I then told him to meet me again at 7 a.m. the next morning. The Tunku who sat next to me when this incident took place told me afterwards with a twinkle in his eye that I should not have behaved in that manner but should have taken the proffered hand. It was arranged for me to visit a cocoa experimental plot at Kampung Sawah, half way between Kuala Lumpur and Kuantan. The officer was at the Rest House, I was told, at 6.45 a.m. I came down from my room at 7.15 wanting purposely to make him wait for fifteen minutes. After this, word went round that I was the 'Unholy terror'. The end result was that I had reduced the potential opposition considerably and no further attempts by expatriate officers at being disrespectful took place. Above all, I got almost whatever I wanted done and always done at speed!

Another officer quite high up in service was to stay for ten years but two years after Merdeka left all of a sudden. He was on the Malayanization Committee and the chief negotiator for the British Government in successfully extracting compensation for expatriate officers to the tune of $100 million to be deposited in the United Kingdom, before 31 August 1957, i.e. the day fixed for Merdeka.

Ultimately he left long before his time was up, because as head of a department I passed him over whenever I required an officer to accompany me during my tour of the country, and requested his deputy, an Irishman, instead. Finally, I recommended the *Johan Mangku Negara* or J.M.N. for this officer, more than appropriate for his rank as a deputy Director. And when the award to the Irishman was announced in the Press the Director felt it no longer possible for him to stay in service and left the country quite soon after.

During the period of Malaya's achieving Merdeka our foreign policy was that it should remain under the umbrella of British advice. The Tunku completely refused to have any truck or connexion with Communist countries, including the U.S.S.R., until ten years after Merdeka. On many occasions I attempted to argue with him on the wisdom of having diplomatic relations with the U.S.S.R. but in vain. One of my common arguments was that 'it is better to come close to someone, even though we suspect him of being the devil. We would then know the devil at close range.' Malaya began to have diplomatic relations with Russia only ten years later for two reasons—one to sell directly our rubber and secondly, according to the Tunku himself, the U.S.S.R. would act as a buffer against Communist China. The fact remains that the Tunku during his Premiership was quite firm in respect of foreign policy and in many other fields as well. In other words he was always a few steps behind current thinking in those early days because of advice he got outside the Cabinet.

On the other hand, whenever I went overseas to Europe, for

example for F.A.O. Conferences, meeting groups of fellow delegates, and since Malaya was outside the Afro-Asian group, I sensed being looked down upon by delegates of those countries. We were considered then to be still under British tutelage and they were right. This feeling of mine emerges because deep in my heart I am pro-Afro-Asian and to be snubbed by them was something I could not really accept.

The souring of relations between the Tunku and myself became a little more advanced after the second election of 1959, when Khir Johari, the then Minister of Education, had to contest the election again because his opponent was found to be of unsound mind and I was asked to act in the Portfolio of Education. I acted for two weeks until the Tunku asked me to give it up and he gave it to Tun Razak. The occasion was a little unusual as I was at that time in hospital for a major operation. Perhaps it was partly my fault for having acted rather bluntly and without consideration as an *acting* Minister when I removed the Head of the newly-formed Language Institute and his deputy, both of them expatriates, from their posts. Also for having changed the name of Malay schools then known as Sekolah Umum to Sekolah Kebangsaan while Khir Johari was still contesting the unfinished election. In the latter case I admitted that I acted hastily. From then on there was nothing more for me, as I was truly in serious trouble with my colleagues. But to all intents and purposes it was the Tunku himself, as the other Ministers did not show their hands openly. During the second election, in 1959, several Ministers asked me to campaign in their constituencies admitting that I had been working on the ground while they perhaps had not been able to spend as much time as they would have liked in their own constituencies. A few months before Nomination Day vast sums of money were made available for rapid-result schemes to be implemented forthwith. I too had neglected my own constituency of Kuala Langat, but spent most of my time in other parts of the country, especially in the East Coast areas, implementing Agricultural co-operatives and also fishing projects. However, I made a statement saying that if my constituents rejected me as a result of my giving priority elsewhere, I would have the satisfaction at least of having concentrated on areas where the people needed more urgent attention than my own voters.

When the election was over, and after leaving hospital for a brief holiday on Penang Hill, I went to Rome to attend the Food and Agricultural Organisation Plenary Sessions. Before leaving, I had several consultations with experts of the Food and Agricultural Organisation regional office from Bangkok to formulate the establishment of a urea fertilizer plant and a paper mill, the latter utilizing as raw material padi straw, which hitherto had been burnt after harvest. The Imperial Chemical Industries of United Kingdom had all this while been supplying the bulk of fertilizer used in Malaya, a virtual monopoly. The idea naturally was a shock to the I.C.I. and after a few months of campaigning throughout the length and breadth of the country, the Tunku asked me if I would consider abandoning it. I said that it had caught on with the people and that it would be difficult to withdraw the project at that stage.

While I was away in Europe the Tunku and Tun Razak began a rural development programme with the Tunku as head, and Tun Razak was given the task of carrying it out. The once well-known 'Red Book' co-ordinated all agricultural efforts to be centralized on the Federal, State, District and Mukim levels and Tun Razak was to direct the operation. An Operations Room at all levels was established similar to the Operations Rooms established during the Emergency to combat the communist terrorists in Malaya. It was inevitable that there were skirmishes between me and Tun Razak, the officials of the Ministry of Agriculture and those of the Ministry of Rural Development. There were bitter exchanges of letters which I retained for the purpose of record, and they are now in the National Archives.

About this time the Cabinet, however, was reluctant to approve my projects, i.e. the urea plant and the paper mill. I did not know then that an earlier commitment with a foreign firm had been made to establish a fertilizer factory. I was later asked if I could satisfy the Cabinet that my project would be in the national interest and supported by the people and also if it was a viable one. If it was, it would then be reconsidered. However, many loyal officers and officials of the Co-operative Societies and Banking Unions informed me of this move by the Commissioner for Co-operative Development to frustrate the efforts of the Ministry. On hearing this I went to see the Tunku and personally reported this officer after taking action to remove him from the Ministry. He was to leave immediately. I then reported to the Tunku what took place subsequently at the Apex Bank General Meeting when the Co-operative Societies and Banking Unions supported unanimously the establishment of a separate Co-operative Fertilizer and Paper Mill Society. The Tunku said that if the people wanted to establish the plant he would not stand in their way, but if they would give up the urea plant, he would find money for the paper mill.

There was clearly bad blood between me and some of my Cabinet colleagues. I then decided for the sake of solidarity in the Party to leave the country. I explained to the Tunku that I would be willing to be posted to an Embassy about to be established in Bonn, which I took a liking to during my tour of Europe. The Tunku when informed of this agreed. But later he changed his mind saying, 'It can't be done, Aziz. I would certainly be accused by the people of sending you away.' Campaigning then went on with redoubled vigour with me stomping the country to explain in detail to the farmers the project by which they could themselves own a fertilizer plant and for which they would get cheaper and unlimited supplies of fertilizer for their padi and other crops.

The Tunku was approached by both I.C.I. and Esso and so was Khir Johari, who was at that time Minister of Commerce and Industry. Neither of these giant organizations as yet had fertilizer plants in the country and they were then about to make an application to establish them. Esso at this time was planning to establish an oil refinery in Port Dickson and by a coincidence had also applied for the same piece of land which the Co-operative Society wanted for its urea plant.

It is important at this stage to give a picture of the position of fertilizers in the country soon after the War. When the farmers were discouraged from using out-dated fertilizers such as bat guano, burnt bones and burnt padi straw, I.C.I. brought in ammonium sulphate. Soon after the Alliance came to power the officers in my Ministry successfully campaigned against the use of these outmoded types of fertilizers. It was discovered that in many areas our soil is acidic and therefore does not respond to the use of ammonium sulphate. The I.C.I. at that time were exporting ammonium sulphate from their factories to other former colonial territories where the soil composition was not the same as in Malaya. As their fertilizer plants were producing only sulphate of ammonia they used their influence with expatriate officials in my Ministry, quite a number of whom were still serving the country, to play down this new magic fertilizer known as urea.

The F.A.O. experts suggested that I should visit several fertilizer plants and paper mills in France, Germany and Italy. Before arriving in Rome in the autumn of 1959 I spent three weeks touring fertilizer factories in these countries. I was accompanied by Jimmy Tang Wai Chin, a private engineering consultant, during my tour. Jimmy was later responsible for preparing the feasibility reports on the urea plant and the paper mill. These reports were later endorsed by F.A.O. consultants. My proposed urea plant and paper mill projects were enthusiastically supported by F.A.O. experts in Rome and the United Nations Technical Assistant experts from New York who reported favourably on the establishment of a urea plant. On my return home a pamphlet was distributed in thousands to the kampungs through co-operative societies and during my own visits.

When I started my campaign for support from the people directly and from co-operative societies, poor though the farmers were and with age-old traditions of prejudices against changes in agricultural practice, within less than six months half a million dollars were collected.

The matter was by no means decided, however. A few months later the Tunku decided to take the matter up at the UMNO Annual General Assembly in Malacca on 6 May 1961. In his presidential address he condemned me for wanting to establish the urea plant and paper mill as not worthy of support by the Government. He quoted figures which showed that he lacked proper information on the trend of world agricultural progress and was quite oblivious of the fact that the figures he gave were given to him by those vested interests themselves rather than by officials within the country. For the first time in the history of the Party, a matter which normally was within the orbit of a Cabinet decision was brought out into the open, at an UMNO General Assembly. After his speech an attempt was made by Selangor delegates, of whom I was chairman, to amend a Motion of Thanks to the Tunku for his presidential speech. It was to delete any reference to the proposed urea plant. This was defeated by 99 votes to 44. However, over 100 delegates abstained from voting. This in fact was tantamount to a defeat for the Tunku.

Perhaps it will be useful for me to give a verbatim report of the *Straits Times* on 8 May 1961:

A Selangor attempt to amend a motion of thanks to Tunku Abdul Rahman for his presidential speech by deleting any reference to the proposed urea fertilizer factory was defeated by 99 to 44 votes at the UMNO General Assembly here today.

This was after a member of the UMNO central executive committee, Encik Abdul Ghafar bin Baba, Malacca's Chief Minister, had warned the meeting that such an amendment was tantamount to a motion of 'no confidence' in the Tunku and the central executive committee.

There was heated debate on the motion which centred around the feasibility of setting up an urea fertilizer factory, during which the Government was warned against falling into the bait of big capitalists.

A Perak delegate, Megat Zainuddin bin Ahmad, chairman of the Kinta Selatan division, walked out of the assembly after he had accused the assembly chairman, Syed Esa bin Alwi, of not giving him any opportunity to speak on the urea factory question. But he returned for the afternoon session.

The 'thank you' motion, moved by Encik Abdul Ghani bin Ishak, read:

'That this assembly thank the national president, Tunku Abdul Rahman, for his speech and notes that every effort will be made to implement the policies contained in the speech.'

Encik Mustapha Yunus, of Ulu Langat, moved an amendment by inserting the words 'with the exception of matters relating to the urea fertilizer factory'.

Encik Abdul Aziz bin Ishak, the Minister of Agriculture and Co-operatives was the first to take the floor when the debate began.

He regretted that the Tunku's speech concerning the urea factory was contrary to Malay public opinion. He explained that the urea factory was a post-war innovation produced mainly from Japan, Germany, Italy and the United States.

Britain had not yet produced the fertilizer.

It was found that soil could absorb the fertilizer more easily than phosphate.

The recent Food and Agriculture Organisation conference in Saigon had held the view that phosphate could become a thing of the past when farmers learnt the value of urea fertilizer.

A United Nations expert, Dr. H.J. Mukerjee, who recently spent ten days in Malaya, recommended the setting-up of the factory.

Encik Aziz said he tried to get Dr. Mukerjee to see the Tunku, but the Tunku was too busy to see him.

He had asked the Tunku to set up an independent committee to inquire into the feasibility of setting up the urea fertilizer factory, but the Tunku refused to do so.

The Tunku, replying, said that in his speech yesterday he said the cost of setting up the factory at $25 million was too high and the Government was not satisfied with the importance of the plan and, therefore, would not give financial support.

The Tunku added that he had also advised that money collected for the factory would be better utilized for setting up a paper factory and a fertilizer agency.

The urea factory plan, the Tunku said, could not ensure 100 per cent success. If assurances of success were obtained and the ra'ayat decided that the factory should be set up, then the plan could go ahead.

The Tunku said that a wrong impression had been given about the Government's attitude towards the urea factory plan.

What he had said in his speech was that the Government could not give the project financial support.

Dato Sheik Ahmad bin Hashim, chairman of the Apex Bank, who is a member of the central executive committee, said that the Apex Bank had withheld support for the venture because it feared a loss.

Haji Abdul Rahman bin Yusof, of Pasir Puteh, Kelantan, described the Tunku's speech as 'pouring cold water on the urea factory project'.

He said the project had received full support from the people and he alone had collected $100,000.

Encik Abdullah bin Haji Mohamed, of Pontian in Johore, said the urea factory project would not only raise the economic position of the Malays, but would also relieve unemployment among the Malays.

He could not understand the Government's attitude in not supporting the project while experts had given it the green light.

What the ra'ayat wanted now was that the Government should give it pioneer status and not to give such status to other companies.

He warned the Government against falling into a capitalist trap.

The strongest opposition to the urea factory plan came from Nik Hassan bin Yahya, a member of the central executive committee.

He claimed that the co-operative ice factory in Kelantan had enriched the Chinese, who were also agents of Cold Storage. He said that the setting up of a urea factory could not give a good investment guarantee.

Encik Mustapha Yunus accused Nik Hassan of spreading poisonous propaganda about the proposed factory.

The 'thank you' motion was passed unanimously.

The Tunku's leadership was challenged and the result was quite obvious, although in the Press there was no mention of abstentions. The shock was so unnerving to the Tunku that the next day he soft-pedalled on the urea plant again, perhaps for the third time.

During the lunch break of the UMNO General Assembly at Malacca, the Selangor delegates joined me for lunch at a restaurant where there was no private room. Special Branch Officers sat at a table nearby and listened to our conversation. From that day onwards I was not left alone, being shadowed everywhere I went. Perhaps the tapping of my telephone also began at about this time and lasted until about ten years later, five years after my release from detention.

Soon after this, in September 1960, the Information Department was given instructions not to handle press releases and other coverage on the fertilizer plant. On hearing this I wrote a letter to the Tunku recalling that in his conversation with me in the previous month he gave me the green light to proceed with my campaign, since he said he would not stand in my way if the people wanted the plant. I mentioned also in the letter that the project should be given the same amount of publicity which was usually accorded to any project supported and backed by the people. I asked for his clarification on this matter and requested that I be told of his exact stand on the project in order to avoid further misunderstanding. No reply was received. In March 1961 I wrote another letter to him, complaining that the Assistant Minister for Information, Syed Jaffar Albar, did not agree to my proposed broadcast over Radio Malaya and also to talks by experts to intensify the campaign on the projects of urea and paper plants. I added that he had already indicated that he had no objection personally. Therefore Albar's reason for not agreeing to the broadcast was that it was a private project and not a Government one. It seemed that the situation was perhaps purposely made confusing for me, in order to frustrate my efforts. To this letter there was again no reply.

On my part I carried on with the campaign and, with the help of F.A.O. experts from Bangkok, where the F.A.O. Regional Headquarters is, proceeded with the plan to establish the urea plant. I made arrangements for the experts to see the Tunku and his economic advisers, but the Tunku did not agree. A feasibility report which was sent ahead to the Prime Minister's Department received no comments, favourable or otherwise. I was therefore placed in a very difficult position, but my faith and determination were unabated. During 1961 a global tender was put out for the building of the plant. Those shortlisted included the well-known firms of fertilizer factory contractors Friedrich Uhde of West Germany, Monte-Cartini of Italy and Simon-Carves of the United Kingdom and Australia. Simultaneously, with the sending of the feasibility report to the Prime Minister's Department a copy was sent through the proper channel to the Government of India in New Delhi to seek their co-operation as an independent party to determine whether or not the project was feasible. Towards the latter part of 1961 the Fertilizer Co-operation of India, a wholly-Government concern, invited me, the Fertilizer Society local experts and four members of the Board of Directors of the Society to visit India for a conference. The trip was a success. We visited a Government fertilizer plant about sixty miles from Calcutta and another near Delhi. The visit was not considered an official one by the Government. It was to the Fertilizer Society. However, we were received in accordance with protocol in India and at a party given for us in Delhi, there were many Indian Government officials who received us at the New Delhi Airport on arrival.

The conference in Calcutta and New Delhi with the experts of the Fertilizer Co-operation of India pronounced our project as sound and feasible. Approval of the Government of India was given for a senior project manager of the organization to come to Kuala Lumpur to help select the most suitable of the tenders. The Prime Minister's Department in Kuala Lumpur had from time to time been briefed on the progress of the proposal but we had no indication in writing of their response.

At this period my life as a Minister in the Malayan Cabinet was anything but happy. I was made to feel almost an outcast by some of my colleagues, especially towards the end of 1961 and the early part of 1962. Many of my other projects, although passed in Parliament, especially those connected with co-operatives, were hindered by the Treasury which would not release monies already voted.

IV. THE RIFT WIDENS

THE Chinese as a race were previously prejudiced against co-operative organizations and preferred private enterprise. Much groundwork had to be done before they realized the benefits of banding themselves together. More and more Chinese officers were recruited to what had in the past been the preserve of Malays. In my time alone many Chinese co-operative societies were being established, including fishermen's societies and ice-plant societies to provide ice for the fishermen. Another society of the Chinese was the successfully-run fishing-gear society, in Malacca. Quite naturally the joint-stock companies who had hitherto had a free run of the business of ice manufacture took exception to the projects of the Ministry of Agriculture.

Perhaps it is not out of place for me to mention that the first Minister of Finance of the Malayan Cabinet, Colonel Sir Henry Lee, was more practical and far-sighted when he took over from the British Colonial Officer, the Secretary to the Treasury. After my request for a thorough and complete reorganization of the Department of Co-operative Development requiring ten times the number of officers to be recruited in a single budget year, he gave his approval. With this new policy, officers of different cadres were being rapidly trained, either overseas or at the new Co-operative College opened just before Independence. The year after, another extension to the wing of the college was added, and yet another was added two years later in order to meet the present commitments and further responsibilities of this branch of rural development. I was, however, in the early days cautioned not to to be over-ambitious and expand too rapidly in the field of co-operative development. Perhaps my outlook was always a little ahead of that of others.

When one has fallen foul with the top, everything one does

rightly or wrongly is labelled wrong. Tan Siew Sin, the Minister of Finance at this time, tried to justify himself when he denied finances for co-operative projects by saying that nearly 2½ million dollars had been given out to Malay fishermen and farmers but the return was slow. He therefore felt justified in stopping further assistance to the rural people.

This was rather a bleak period for me as a Cabinet Minister when from all angles I was being hemmed in. I realized I was already *persona non grata*.

He objected in the Cabinet to my proposed visit to attend the Afro-Asian conference on Rural Reconstruction in Cairo as not worth being attended by Malaya. He somehow had the idea that the Afro-Asian line-up was something unholy. I had to give an assurance to my colleagues that no communist-controlled countries would be represented there. It was the first time that Malaya had been represented at any Afro-Asian conference. Hitherto any mention of the Afro-Asian Organisation by me inside or outside the Cabinet would result in a guffaw and side glances. The idea of having anything to do with the Afro-Asian Organisation at that time was considered a waste of time. It was not until 1965, after my arrest, when the Afro-Asian countries held a meeting in Algiers, that the Malaysian Government realized how important the Afro-Asian relationship is to an Asian country like Malaysia.

However, a small delegation of three, including myself as leader, attended the conference in March 1962. One was the Assistant Commissioner of Co-operatives, the other was a State Agricultural Officer. In Cairo, between sessions, I was able to relax and to take stock of the situation *vis-à-vis* my colleagues and myself, and I found that it was not possible to carry on working as a Minister in the Cabinet. I was in a detached atmosphere in Cairo, able to write on several personal subjects pertaining to my Ministry. This included the urea project, giving the Tunku the latest development in the pious hope that if he did not read the feasibility report sent to him earlier and those official letters, at least he would read my personal ones. I also mentioned that it would be useful and timely to hold the next meeting of the Afro-Asian Organisation on Rural Reconstruction in Kuala Lumpur. I stressed that it was an effective organization for mutual economic co-operation in Afro-Asian countries whose problems did not differ very much. The part of my letter to the Tunku that made him decide to invite the Afro-Asian countries to hold the conference in Kuala Lumpur and which impressed him most was that Afro-Asian countries were keen to know more of our plans and programmes, and if the conference was held in Malaya it would be a valuable mouthpiece for our efforts in the field of rural development. This, I added, would forestall attempts by the Opposition in the forthcoming elections to minimize the work done by our Government. Paradoxically, I was in the Opposition in the 1964 elections and lost my Parliamentary seat.

On my return to Kuala Lumpur at the beginning of April, I held several meetings with the Fertilizer and Paper Mill Society before the arrival of the promised experts from the Fertilizer Corporation of India to examine and award the contract to build the plant. After my press conference on the day after my arrival in Kuala Lumpur, I was wearing an Egyptian national dress which had been presented to me in Cairo, complete with decorated skull-cap. The next morning the *Straits Times* carried a large picture of me, and the report of the conference in Cairo. The Tunku was with the ASA leaders in Cameron Highlands. On my return home after a reception given by Dr. Mohd. Razif, the Indonesian ambassador in Kuala Lumpur, in honour of Dr. Hatta, the former Vice-President of Indonesia, a telegram was awaiting me. It was from the Tunku. It read: 'Aziz Ishak; Minister of Agriculture, Kuala Lumpur. Having seen your picture I am convinced that everything is not right with you. Perhaps a medical board might examine your sanity. Signed Tunku Abdul Rahman.' I was not sure whether the telegram was meant as a joke or the reverse, it had a little venom in it.

However, I sent a phonogramme addressed to him at Cameron Highlands at 10 p.m. that evening. 'Thank you very much for your telegram stop. Perhaps we are in the same boat stop. Shall wait at the railway station Monday morning and we might play golf first time.' It transpired that the Tunku before sending the telegram to me showed its text to his V.I.P. guests. They were, I was told, very amused, but when he received my reply he was sporting enough to show it to them. They were again amused.

Next morning I received news from Cameron Highlands that a domesticated deer which I had found trapped in the compound of the agricultural station at Cameron Highlands three years earlier when it was a month old had been sacrificed for a venison satay party. It was said that the Tunku, after sending out trappers in Cameron Highlands to hunt for deer had failed, and resorted to the slaughter of a pet animal. On Monday morning, as promised, I waited for the Tunku at the Kuala Lumpur railway station and went in his official car to his residence. We discussed the impending meeting with the Board of Directors of the Fertilizer Society at which a decision would be taken. Then the Tunku suggested that a joint participation of the urea plant would meet his agreement with Esso holding 51% and co-operatives and other local capital 49%. I promised him that the matter would be seriously considered by the Board. If this could be agreed to he would support the project. Also the Fertilizer Society would be given sole distribution rights to market the products.

The meeting of the full Board began before dinner at the Ministry of Agriculture and lasted until 2 a.m. I tried to use what influence I could muster to persuade the Board to accept Tunku Abdul Rahman's formula of joint participation with Esso. It was, however, unanimously resolved to go it alone. The Board decided to award the contract to Friedrich Uhde of Germany at a cost of 26 million dollars. The plant would produce 100 tons of urea per day or 60 tons of liquid ammonia per day at about the current price of urea at that time. The interest rate was 6%. The scheme of payment was that 10% should be paid on signing the contract and 10% when shipment of machinery and equipment was completed. The balance would be paid up after the plant commenced production within a period of seven years by instalments. The plant would be in production twenty-four months after execution of the contract. The society, however, at the time of signing the contract had insufficient funds to pay the initial 10% required. Uhde had asked for a Government guarantee, failing which a bank guarantee. But since Tunku Abdul Rahman did not agree to a Government guarantee, I approached several commercial banks in the country to underwrite the balance of the loan. This, however, hit a snag. The Bank Negara which controls the granting of loans by the commercial banks was reluctant with its guarantee. Three days after the award was made to Uhde, with the attendant disappointments and frustrations, I was admitted to hospital because of a heart condition. The contract with Uhde was therefore signed on my hospital bed. That was the end of the project to establish a urea plant.

When I was away in Cairo, it was decided at a Cabinet meeting to transfer me to the Ministry of Health. I was not informed of this until one week after my return, when Cabinet papers of three earlier meetings were sent to me. I refused to accept the transfer. The reasons were that my work was not completed, and also the manner in which I was asked to go to another Ministry without the normal courtesy of being consulted beforehand.

There was bitter correspondence between me and the Tunku who left for the United Kingdom a few days later for the final consultation with the United Kingdom Government on the formation of Malaysia. Newspaper reports from overseas indicated that the Tunku, while in London, was the guest of the Chairman of the Board of Directors of the I.C.I.

While I was away in Cairo other things also happened which sealed my fate as Minister of Agriculture. One was that Tan Siew Sin, the Minister of Finance, sent a paper to the Cabinet on the difficulties and problems affecting my co-operative projects. On my return I put up my comments in great detail to defend those schemes in which I stressed that the co-operative projects were meant to alleviate the hardship of rural communities in the country. At no time were they designed as profit-making projects. If the loans to the co-operatives were slow in coming back, it was quite a normal thing to happen. Malaya was comparatively much better off in this respect compared with co-operatives in India and Ceylon. Finally, I insisted that even if the loans were not returned at all, which was not the case, it would not be money going down the drain. Co-operative members would benefit from the programmes and also would be trained, so that they would stand on their own feet eventually.

Soon after I left the Government in early 1963, Tan Siew Sin and the Tunku accused me of having appropriated to my own use those monies which were paid to the co-operative societies as loans.

If I had converted to my personal use even $10 and not to say $2½ million I would not escape prosecution in court. Also it had been openly admitted by senior officials of Government that in terms of integrity while a Minister for seven-and-a-half years until my resignation my file in the anti-corruption department was a 'blank sheet of paper'.

Finally, perhaps the straw that broke the camel's back was my project in padi marketing. This started a few years earlier in Selangor and Malacca, and continued as a complete project in Krian in Perak. This project was for the first Co-operative Marketing Scheme in Krian. The scheme was started during the harvest of 1961 after one-third of it had been implemented, meanwhile giving an extra profit of three million dollars to some 17,000 farmers, instead of the profit going to the pockets of middlemen. While I was away the Tunku directed that these projects be discontinued and 150 middlemen be asked to continue buying padi in that area. If the scheme had been allowed to continue, the padi farmers that year would have gained an extra $10 million. It was obvious that co-operative organization in Malaya was given only lip-service.

Less than two years after Merdeka I made a speech in Parliament in which I tried to impress the fact that our country's 'Independence so far achieved has been merely political, we have yet to achieve other aspects of it, such as economic, scientific and technological, before we can really claim to be fully independent'.

This part of my speech was not understood at that time by many in the House; but thirteen years later the phrase 'science and technology' caught on *ad nauseam*.

In early 1962 I wrote a letter to Tunku Abdul Rahman, as the new Chancellor of the University of Malaya, after a discussion with him on the need to place greater emphasis on technical education not only at Trade and Technical school level but at Polytechnic and University level.

What I had in mind, of course, were the technicians to service the industries, such as the fertilizer plant and the paper mill and those in the private sector. I recalled in the letter that no newly-independent country could progress satisfactorily unless and until its nationals had attained a certain degree of technological and scientific competence. I pointed out that there was a conspicuous absence of a Department of Industrial Chemistry and Chemical Engineering at the University of Malaya. The continued denial of training facilities in these fields meant that the country had to import high-level technicians for our growing industries, which for many years to come would be at the mercy of foreign technologists. I further recalled in the letter that I had met Sir Alexander Oppenheim, the Vice-Chancellor of the University of Malaya, earlier and emphasized that very same point.

In the letter I then stressed the fact that it was not the policy of the metropolitan powers to introduce such subjects for the simple reason that the former colonies and emerging countries were meant to be suppliers of raw materials and therefore not to take part in industrial development. In this I quoted cases of universities in India, Ceylon, Singapore and those in African territories and the West Indies, but in contrast in the universities of white Commonwealth countries, courses in chemistry were provided. To stress my point further, the reason for this was because the University of Malaya had its development controlled by expatriate officers, so that our country would continue to be merely a supplier of raw materials. My letter to the Tunku closed with a suggestion that 'Since we are already behind time and our industrial programme has gone forward without the necessary permanent bases in the form of University courses in industrial chemistry and chemical technology and a polytechnic, the following lines of action need to be taken:

(1) As many Colombo Plan Scholarships [as possible] in Industrial Chemistry, Chemical Technology be asked from friendly countries. Training should also be requested from United States, France, Germany, Italy and Belgium.

(2) That the University be asked without delay to look into the possibility of starting courses in Industrial Chemistry, Chemical Technology and Chemical Engineering at an early date.

(3) That early steps be taken to set up a Polytechnic to provide for courses not now provided at the Technical Colleges.'

The Tunku, however, merely passed on my letter to the Vice-Chancellor, whose reply sounded to me very much like an apology for things not done rather than a full realization of the urgency of the matter. It contained no indication of positive action to correct the deficiency. My comment on Sir Alexander's letter was also sent to the Tunku.

So far as I know not even today has a full Department of Industrial Chemistry and Chemical Engineering been established.

V. A BRIEF PERIOD AS AN INDEPENDENT MEMBER OF PARLIAMENT

DURING the period when I was no longer a member of the Alliance in Parliament, for a few months before Parliament was prorogued, I took quite an active part during the long Budget Session to clarify my position as an independent member. Taking advantage of the time available I endeavoured to point out cases where the Government had failed to act on matters such as rubber replanting, where contractors supplying replanting material palmed off on innocent Malay smallholders inferior and low-yielding young rubber plants instead of the best material for replanting. The end result of this was that when the new smallholders' rubber was tapped, the yield per acre was not 1,000 to 1,500 pounds as expected, but rather less than the 500 pounds they used to get from their old trees. These remarks of mine found ready support from the back-benchers of the ruling party. I don't propose to quote speeches I made in Parliament during the brief period as an independent member, but, however, managed to rebut accusations from the Tunku against my person on such issues as my personal integrity and sense of responsibility when I was a Minister. Except for a few topmost leaders, no other ranking figures of the Alliance made any attack on me.

When it was finally agreed between the Tunku and me that I would withdraw from the Cabinet I wanted my 'retirement' to be classified as sacked. At first he did not agree to this but he relented later on and at the same time warned me that if sacked I would be disbarred from future employment in his Government. To this, I bluntly said, 'If I wanted a job with you, I would not have left your Government.' After this there was an exchange of letters on the subject in which willy-nilly he agreed to my being sacked.

In early January 1963 when my .three months leave before

retirement was over, I crossed the floor from the Government bench to the opposite side. At this stage I was publicly expelled from the Alliance for contravening party discipline. A week later, at a meeting of Members of Parliament of the Opposition parties held at the Hotel Majestic, I was invited to chair its first meeting. As far as I can recall, Dr. Lim Chong Eu, now Penang's Chief Minister, Datuk S.P. Seenivasagam of the People's Progressive Party, Dr. Tan Chee Khoon of the Labour Party, later the Socialist Front, were unanimous in wanting me to lead the united opposition. The Pan-Malayan Islamic Party, however, although present, made it clear that they were there merely as observers. It is important for me to record here that at no time during the period of my leave did I hold meetings with opposition leaders either openly or secretly until I was no longer receiving my Minister's emolument. I spent my leave in Morib, where I had secured a piece of land about one quarter of an acre in size for the site of my new home. The District Officer in Kuala Langat, my own constituency, was very helpful in speeding up my application for this Government land on the beach. This man of great integrity later tried to help me in more ways than one to put me on my feet in business. But God had other plans for me. In Morib, I built a $4,500/- home of treated timber from the Department of Forestry but did not complete full payment for it until ten years later.

The Opposition leaders met several times during the next six months at premises in Cross Street, provided by the Gerakan, also at the home of a well-known Chinese lawyer. During the six months as chairman, attempts to get the Opposition united were not by any means easy, as ideologically the parties differed. However, we managed from time to time to agree on common objectives, such as to hold joint rallies, and when the Alliance announced the target date for the birth of Malaysia which embraced Singapore, North Borneo and Sarawak, the United Opposition sent a memorandum to the United Nations to protest not because it objected to the plan but rather to the manner in which it was being implemented, stressing the unholy haste with which it was being undertaken. The Opposition suggested that the formation of Malaysia be deferred for two years. The protest was personally handed to Mr. Narasimhan, an Assistant Secretary to U Thant, the United Nations Secretary-General, who happened to be in Kuala Lumpur. Mr. Narasimhan, whom I knew when I was in the Cabinet, seemed rather distant and unfriendly when the United Opposition delegation met him in his suite at the Hotel Merlin. I was the spokesman. But when I made a little introductory speech, the gist of which was earlier agreed to by members of the delegation, and in the presence of the United Nations representative, D.R. Seenivasagam, the Secretary-General of the P.P.P., was challenged by Mr. Narasimhan who commented that the Opposition did not seem to be speaking in one voice.

For me that was the end of my role as chairman of the United Opposition. Some weeks previous to this incident, however, the Deputy President of the Pan-Malayan Islamic Party at one of our meetings, discussing the appointment of an official leader of the Opposition to be submitted to the Speaker of the Dewan Ra'ayat, objected to my name being put up. He remarked that since I did not represent anybody, I did not qualify to represent the Opposition. I took the hint that day and refused to preside at any further meeting but continued to be present as a member.

This was the period when I was rather undecided whether to give up politics completely as the result of the humiliating treatment I had received. A feeling of uncertainty about the wisdom of pursuing politics further was again seriously arising in my mind. No doubt this feeling was also the result of my taking a deep interest in religion and a considerable time is required for this interest to develop.

When a person falls from grace it is inevitable that some of his friends should show sympathy, but not tactfully enough in my case. Very often I was told that I should not have done this or that. And this sudden spate of advice on the part of these well-meaning friends tended to imply that I no longer had any faculty of thinking correctly. Advice was also freely offered by club stewards, former clerks and even a peon or two, not to mention my former Heads of Department who used to consider me a person of intellect, but appeared to imply that I had lost my sense of perspective now that I was no longer a Cabinet Minister.

The target-hitting remarks of the late Encik Zulkifli Mohamed, the Deputy President of the P.M.I.P., were partly responsible for my half-hearted determination to form a party of my own. Later, however, he directed his party members to assist me in my constituency during the election of 1964. The late Encik Zulkifli did at one time suggest that I join his party but I felt unable to do so because I was afraid of an adverse reaction from his party-members. The few loyal friends I had formed the nucleus of the National Convention Party. At the outset I realised that the party could not get along very far without sufficient finances, although its constitution, based on Socialist lines, was attractive and dynamic enough. Among the office bearers were Dr. Syed Husin bin Ali, then a lecturer at the University of Malaya, and Dahari Ali, now chief news editor of the *New Straits Times*. There were a handful of old sincere friends on the Committee and also others less than genuine. The latter were either earlier dropouts from UMNO, while one or two after having passed party security screening, worked as 'spies' for the Government, or those who were convinced by the Minister of Finance's accusation that I had run away with the Co-operative till and wanted to share the booty. On the whole it was a sad situation when the 1964 general election came about in March and the NCP was not by any means ready for it. Apart from contributions from friends through Syed Husin and others, I sold my new Mercedes-Benz diesel-model for $11,000/– and purchased a new Austin Cambridge diesel for less than half the amount realized. The balance of the money went to the kitty of the Party. My wife voluntarily sold all her jewellery and gave me the proceeds amounting to $8,000/–. This also went to the party.

An approach was later made by the Socialist Front to join forces with them on condition that the NCP use the symbol (head of a wild bull or *banteng* supported by tools for agriculture, coloured red). In return for this, the Socialist Front would provide all printing materials and vehicles and other equipment, some items free of charge while others would be paid for. Also, the NCP would pay for candidates' deposits and expenses from nomination day onwards. Finally we fielded six Selangor State Assembly candidates and another six for Pahang. My loyal friend Datuk Kampo Radjo and myself contested both Parliament and State Assembly seats. Our two candidates in Perak, however, switched their loyalty when told that the NCP could only afford to pay for the deposits but not expenses. The result was that none of the NCP candidates was returned.

VI. AFRO-ASIAN SUMMIT
IN CAIRO, 1964

THE Chairman of the Socialist Front, concurrently the elected President of City Council, Malacca, Hasnul Abdul Hadi, and I left for Cairo in July 1964 to attend the Cairo Conference of Non-Aligned Nations as observers. We were not invited to the Conference but as a socialist organization we hoped to receive an invitation when we arrived in Cairo.

The Ambassador of the United Arab Republic in Kuala Lumpur was quite friendly with me when I was still in the Government, so when I called at his Embassy for visas for both of us to go to the Conference, he was very helpful and personally arranged for the visas to be given, and given gratis. In conversation with me while waiting for the visas he confessed that he was unable to understand the attitude of our Government *vis-à-vis* Israel. Although Malaysia, and Malaya before that, had no diplomatic relations with Israel, he was well aware of the frequent visits of the Israeli diplomat from Bangkok to see the Tunku. Also he told me that Malaya was buying quite a considerable amount of Haifa oranges, 'of all the countries in the world producing oranges, why should Malaya import them from Haifa, and yet Malaya wanted to be friendly with the Arab countries?' he asked. I had no suitable reply. After partaking of morning coffee he wished me God speed to visit Egypt. He, however, could not help me to get an invitation to attend the Conference but suggested that a cable be sent to the Conference Secretariat. This we did. We left for Cairo with credentials from the Socialist Front Secretariat in Kuala Lumpur and arrived at 9 p.m. and to our consternation were quarantined because our International Health Certificates were not in order. Peninsular Malaya at this time was declared a cholera-infected area and my own certificate required that I was to be in quarantine for four days while Hasnul's was for six. The Conference, however, was to begin two days after our arrival. Desperate telephone calls were made to various friends in Cairo from the 'Health Hotel' as the place was known. These were in vain. My former opposite number, the Minister of Agriculture of the United Arab Republic, was away on tour, so I was informed. The Malaysian Ambassador to the United Arab Republic when contacted by telephone could not get us out while in quarantine. He, however, sounded neutral, although I knew him well when he was Head of the Chancery in London a few years earlier. He is now the Yang di-Pertuan Besar, Negeri Sembilan. It cost each of us $1 Egyptian per meal for the period of our stay though no charge for accommodation was made.

Upon my release from quarantine I was advised by the health officer-in-charge to go to the Conference Secretariat to present my credentials. After going through what seemed to me unending security checks I found myself with the Chief Security Officer after a long wait of nearly two hours. Then came the process of being grilled by two other young political officers before being sent to meet another at the Hotel Hilton where the Conference was being held.

This official was clearly in a position to admit me to the Conference or to refuse. Since I arrived at the Secretariat without first arranging any accommodation I was unable to give him my Cairo address, but promised to let him know as soon as I checked in at a hotel. For nearly two hours I was hotel hunting and was finally directed to a ship on the Nile where accommodation was available. Many tourists from Europe were also accommodated on board this floating hotel, which at other times plied from Cairo to Aswan and Luxor and back. Wasting no time I telephoned from on board ship to the official concerned at the Hilton. I was asked to see him the next day, which I did, and to my utter disappointment he was unable to give me a firm reply whether or not Hasnul and I could be admitted to the Conference. It was obvious we were suspects, as Malaysia was. He told me to wait for his call at my floating hotel, and that was the last I heard from him. I was, however, given a pass to the Secretariat. When Hasnul came out from quarantine, we went together to the Secretariat and met another official who said that the person named on the card would be unable to see us. That ended any further attempt to get into the Conference.

The day I left 'Hotel Quarantine', Hashim Hassan, a senior officer of the Ministry of Information, arrived in Cairo, only to be detained in the same place. He met Hasnul, but was still kept until the normal period of enforced quarantine was over, despite intervention by the Malaysian Ambassador. After staying for one more night at the floating hotel, we got other accommodation at Hotel Longchamp, close to Cairo's diplomatic enclave. In this hotel we met an Indonesian by chance, who later became the link-man to introduce us to the former Indonesian Ambassador in Kuala Lumpur before the Confrontation of Malaysia with Indonesia. The Ambassador was prepared to sponsor our admission to the Conference although there were only a few days left before it was over, but we declined the offer. Hasnul, meantime, had met the former Algerian Ambassador to Indonesia and concurrently to Malaysia, he was also ready to get us into the Conference as observers, but it was a little too late. We later found out that our telegram sent to the Conference Secretariat in Cairo never arrived.

Meanwhile the cloak and dagger boys of the Malaysian Embassy in Cairo were desperately trying to locate us but found us only as I was leaving Cairo for Jeddah to perform *Umrah*, a minor Haj, performed outside the Haj season. Hasnul, however, left for Algiers and thence for Paris. He succeeded in making useful contacts for the forthcoming Afro-Asian Consultative Committee Conference in Algiers, two years later. The Malaysian Government, however, remained suspect and it was not until the very last moment in 1966, when I was still in detention, that Musa Hitam, now Minister of Primary Industries, managed to make contact with the Afro-Asian Secretariat.

From Jeddah I waited in Karachi for Hasnul's return and then we separated again, I to New Delhi and he back home. In New Delhi I was received at the official residence of the former Indian Minister of Agriculture, then holding the Portfolio of Railways. We had dinner together.

When in Karachi I was approached by a minor official of the Indonesian Embassy in Karachi who suggested that I should wait for a person who was a Member of Parliament from the Republic of Indonesia who would like to meet me. But I did not meet this man, who was on his way to Europe, until I was about to embark for Bangkok at the New Delhi airport on my way home. This emissary from Jakarta asked me to remain in Bangkok for one week, as he had an important message for me which he would convey on his return from Europe. I described this man during my interrogation, but I could not recall his name, being rather Javanese-sounding, though he was quite personable, tall and fair, about forty years old. In Karachi I spent my time doing the usual package tour of the city, but otherwise most of my time was spent studying the copy of the text, translation and commentary of the Holy Koran by Abdullah Yusuf Ali, which I bought in Karachi. From that moment as a proud possessor of the Holy Book I did not waste time on other pursuits.

My stay in Bangkok was only for three days in order to ensure that the Government had no intention of detaining me on my arrival in Penang. In Bangkok, I spoke to our Ambassador, Encik Yaacob Latiff, now Mayor of Kuala Lumpur, and point-blank asked him if there was any desire on the part of the Government to arrest me on my return. He was certain that there was no such intention. I also informed Yaacob that throughout my visit to Cairo and other places, although I met certain people I did not conspire with anyone. Yaacob then said, 'It is best that way.' I then borrowed from him $150/– to pay my hotel bill and after speaking to Hasnul on the telephone at his home in Malacca, I left for home.

Incidentally the trip cost me personally $1,000/–, apart from my other expenses paid for by Hasnul, such as hotel bills in Cairo and Karachi. Both our air tickets were secured by invoice and paid for a few weeks after our return by Socialist Front leaders.

Returning home after being away for a month, I carried on as usual, not thinking about politics. My time was spent among the ordinary kampung people in a typical kampung way of life. The Holy Koran became the centre of my attention. I studied its contents with keenness and inspired awe. However, one evening my friend Datuk Kampo Radjo came with two other friends asking me to go to Kuala Lumpur to meet an Indonesian agent who very much wanted to talk to me. I told Datuk Kampo frankly that I was not interested in meeting anyone, as I had decided to keep away from politics. I related how my trip to Cairo with Hasnul was anything but successful and that my temperament would no longer tolerate being further exploited by anyone. I quoted instances where Hasnul and I did not get along during the trip and that ideologically I seemed to have lost faith in socialism. Datuk Kampo pleaded with me to see this mysterious agent. Not wanting to disappoint him I went. In Kuala Lumpur the person I met was not an Indonesian agent at all, he was in fact a reporter from the *Utusan Melayu*, an agent nevertheless, but from an unidentified organization. The moment I saw him I was certain something was dramatically wrong. It was a trap. On the pretext of wanting a vast sum of money to leave for my family, before I was ready to leave the country, he brought one-sixth the amount I asked for, and then I found out the truth. I refused to have anything more to do with him and left for home by bus. After my arrival in Penang I was again persuaded through the telephone to reconsider accepting the plan to leave for any place I chose for the purpose of forming a Malayan Government in Exile. When I refused, there the matter ended. During the interrogation while in detention I suggested that the whole idea came from the Special Branch of the Police and was created for the sole purpose of trapping me and the others.

PART I

Tis strange but true : for truth is always strange—
Stranger than fiction!

BYRON, *Don Juan*

I. ARREST

IT was seven o'oclock on a bright sunny morning during Ramadan, the fasting month for all Muslims in Malaysia. Before dawn I had risen from my morning prayer, and then, until the sun began to come up over the rim of the sea, I read the Koran, as it was my habit to do.

Calm in mind, content in my heart, I went downstairs, picking up a Malacca cane for my morning stroll, as was my custom. In the kitchen I could hear my wife and children happily busy making the cakes they love for the Hari Raya festival, only a few days away. To anyone who knows Malaysia and the Malays well, Hari Raya is the most joyful time of the year. Weeks before the two-day festival every Malay house is alive with happy expectancy, growing more so each day, as everyone looks forward to the open-house hospitality to celebrate the ending of the Fast.

My home at Batu Maung is on a rocky hill-top above a quiet village on the south coast of the island of Penang. As I stepped outdoors, white ripples ran on the blue water before the sea-breeze, the warm wind blew the fronds of all the palm trees down below, nodding and rustling in the morning air. Swinging my cane, a smile on my face, I took my familiar path down the hill to the fishermen's landing-place where I used to call early each day to look at the boats coming in with their night-hauls from the open sea. It was always a pleasant sight, often quite exciting to watch, as the fishermen, eager for home, hastened in to be the first to beach. I didn't have a care in the world. It was just another happy day.

While waiting for the boats, still some distance out, no sails now, only the hum of their outboard motors, I stopped at a little street stall where my old friend, Omar, was making coffee and tea for the fishermen, a few of them Malays, who were unable to fast; others were non-Malays coming in. I greeted him cheerfully and picked up his copy of *Warta Negara*, the local Malay newspaper. The front page had big headlines and a spread of photographs. I stood astonished; they were people I knew well, including my friend, Datuk Kampo Radjo, a fellow-member of the National Convention Party. He had been arrested! Quickly I read on, and this is what I learned:

Hari Raya Idil Fitri Eve Arrests. Four Leaders Suspected of Being Involved in Recruiting Personnel for Training in Indonesia Rounded up. Political Leaders Held.

KUALA LUMPUR, 27 January: Four political leaders suspected of being involved in recruiting personnel for training in Indonesia have been arrested by the Police.

These Hari Raya Idil Fitri Eve arrests were made in the interests of the peace and security of the country and the nation.

Among those arrested was Encik Hussain Yaakub, a member of the Editorial Staff of *Utusan Melayu*, Head Office, Kuala Lumpur.

Three more persons, Datuk Raja Abu Hanifah, PMIP (Pan Malayan Islamic Party) Election Supervisor; Datuk Kampo Radjo, Acting General Secretary of Party Perhimponan Kebangsaan (National Convention Party), which is led by Encik Aziz Ishak, former Minister of Agriculture; and Encik Rais Annuar.

In a statement today, the Government emphasised that these men were involved in recruiting and sending several Malays to Indonesia for guerilla and subversion training.

When these trainees returned they would be utilised to foment an uprising among local inhabitants, and so begin an armed revolution. Several of these trainees, however, were captured. According to information from four of the trainees arrested they were to form a Reception Committee for Indonesian intruders.

The Government further stated that in the interest of the peace and security of the country and the nation, the Government felt that its duty was to take action against them.

In the meantime, Datuk Dr. Ismail, Minister of Home Affairs, when confirming the Police action, said that these people were arrested and not detained.

I quickly read through this item of news. At first it did not startle me, but later it reacted slowly on my mind. I sensed a feeling of bafflement, but I was not unduly disturbed by it. However, I did not read it more than once as I did not feel like doing so again. I did not even buy the paper, but left for home, and when I got there I did not realize that I had already reached it. Such was the condition of my mind at the time. On arriving home I quietly told my wife, Wan Shamsiah, about the news but she seemed quite unperturbed.

I had moved from my home in Morib, which is in Kuala Langat, Selangor, this being my former Parliamentary Constituency. The move took place after I lost the election in March 1964. I had started building my house at Batu Maung one year earlier, but it was not ready until after the election.

Perhaps it was because I felt I was not involved and had turned down an offer to go overseas, that I did not really expect to receive a visit from the police. It was in fact a conflict of the sub-conscious mind. I knew that I was not guilty in the true sense of the word.

That same afternoon, at 5.40 p.m. a posse of police in plain-clothes and in uniform, about twenty in all, suddenly turned up at my home, and with a screeching of brakes of Land-Rovers and motor-cars, surrounded the house. The party was in the charge of Mr. Chan Ah Chan, Deputy Superintendent of Police, whom I knew. I did not know the others, but later I recognized an officer in plain-clothes as the brother of Encik Henry Putra, my old colleague and friend in office when I was Minister of Agriculture, 1955–63.

When the police arrived I was upstairs reading the Koran. I had done such reading daily for the past two-and-a-half months. I was in the middle of Surah *Fath*, meaning Victory. It was indeed a spiritual victory as the Surah aptly referred to the Treaty of Hudaibiya. Under this Treaty the pagan Meccan Quraish, after many years of unrelenting conflict with Islam, at length recognized Islam as an equal power with themselves. In fact this Treaty opened the doors for the spread of Islam throughout Arabia, and thence throughout the world. In another respect God, by this Treaty, had opened a spiritual door for me as a student of Islam. In the Surah, any mistakes of the past were to be rectified and any further mistakes—major ones, of course—prevented. I truly believed in this!

The police were rather impatient while I was searching for the key to my front door. They had already seen me peeping out of my window upstairs when they first arrived. In fact, in a hazy kind of way, I rather expected them; why, I can't explain. When I managed at last to open the front door, the delay had been no more than two minutes, but it might have seemed very much longer to them. Ah Chan informed me quite respectfully that I was under arrest, and asked me to get dressed.

After inviting them into the house, I called to my wife in the kitchen to keep calm as the time had arrived for me to go away. Perhaps my tranquillity of bearing reassured her. She did not cry; perhaps she was too shocked!

I asked the police to sit down in the hall upstairs, saying that we could talk about the whole affair there without any excitement. The only officer in uniform was an Inspector who, in fact, was detailed to carry out the arrest officially. I told Ah Chan that I had known him at the time when he was among other police officers who acted as Royal tombak-bearers during official cere-monies in Kuala Lumpur at the Istana Negara, His Majesty's Palace. He was rather surprised that I remembered him. After this remark, his already respectful attitude towards me became even more so. Although in plain-clothes he almost came close to clicking his heels when speaking to me. After all he was only human; on my part I reciprocated with equal grace. After the police officers had made themselves comfortable, I asked Ah Chan if I could be given a little time, as I would like to break my fast and perform my evening prayer before being taken away. He readily agreed.

I then asked, 'Am I to be taken from Penang, and if so, where to?'

He replied, 'Kuala Lumpur.'

'By what mode of transport?'

'You are going by the Night Mail,' he answered.

Having heard previously that detainees were usually handcuffed when being taken to their destination, I asked him if this would be so in my case. Hesitatingly he nodded his head. I then suggested he could do me a favour by contacting his superior officer in Kuala Lumpur to ask if I could be taken there without causing embarrassment to me, as I did not want to be handcuffed, open to public gaze, during the trip by train. Would it not be better by car? Ah Chan said he would go back to his office in Penang to seek permission for me to go by car. He came back about half an hour later with my request granted. Instead of returning to Penang, I was sure that he must have telephoned from the police station at Bayan Lepas, only a few miles away, otherwise he would have taken more like an hour to come back, not half an hour. He said I was to be taken by a plain-clothes officer in his own car accompanied by three plain-clothes detectives.

By this time it was already 6.30 p.m. I then went downstairs to tell my wife and two of my children what was happening. My son, Zulkifli, who lived with us, had gone to see my eldest daughter, Rahmah, who was in the Penang General Hospital, having been a patient there for the past three months with a chest complaint.

I told my wife of the plan to go to Kuala Lumpur by car and asked her to be calm and not to cry. She was to telephone her father in Kuala Lumpur, and her brother, Wan Yahya bin Pawan Teh, the President of the Sessions Court in Taiping, Perak, to inform them of my arrest. Perhaps Wan Yahya could come with his wife from Taiping which was not so far away (only fifty-three miles) to be with her and console her. My wife managed to control her emotions until nearly the time for me to leave the house. All this while she was in the kitchen preparing for the *buka puasa* (breaking of the fast), making *laksa lemak* and *ketas2*, a pulut-flour cake encrusted in sugar.

I found that I had only $6, which was to last until my remittance arrived from Singapore at the end of the month—in two days' time. Looking out of the window I saw that my friend and neighbour, Mr. Soong Min Thau, had already arrived home from Penang. I informed Ah Chan that I wanted to call him and leave certain instructions about my home and family. Min Thau came over, and I told him that in the event of my wife deciding to move away from Penang, after consulting all my children and her brothers, the house was to be rented furnished for a period of not less than a year at a time. I also said that I only had $6 and asked him to lend me some money. He took out his purse and found he had $40; he gave me all of it saying, 'If you want more I can easily get it from my house.' I thanked him warmly, and said I did not want any more.

I then asked him to allow my wife to telephone her father and her brother from his house. He agreed. I was told later that Wan Yahya, my brother-in-law, was rather embarrassed that his name was mentioned in the newspapers the next day 'as the brother of my wife, contacted by phone as instructed by me'.

I can understand his feelings, as after all he had a judicial position as President of the Sessions Court. It was obvious that this bit of information must have been leaked to the Press by one of the police officers who overheard my private conversation with my wife. Subsequently I heard that Wan Yahya protested to a Senior Assistant Commissioner of Police (Special Branch) about this leakage and the coupling of his name with mine during the arrest. The police officer promised to investigate the leakage, but that was the last he heard of it. It could not have been an ordinary Detective Police Constable (D.P.C.) who had given the leak.

Meantime, I started to pack. I took along with me a translation of the Koran by Abdullah Yusuf Ali; also one bottle of hair cream, one dozen tooth-brushes, about a dozen cakes of toilet soap, tubes of tooth-paste, etc., enough to last for a few months. I asked Ah Chan if I could also take a new blanket. Later on this was to prove useful, as no blanket was provided at my second place of detention. He had no objection. In my haste, I packed only two shirts, but half-a-dozen pairs of trousers.

The police party searched my room and examined stacks of files and documents, but they removed nothing. I was afraid that some of my personal files, with letters exchanged between me and the Prime Minister and my former colleagues in the Cabinet, would be confiscated. But this did not happen.

When the time came for me to break my fast at 7.00 p.m. I went downstairs to the dining-room. I had no appetite. I had to force myself to eat what normally was my favourite dish—the *laksa lemak*. I had only a few spoonfuls and talked to my family more than I ate. This was the last opportunity I had to speak with my wife and children and have a meal together. In the event it was to be a long time before we sat at our own table again. Meanwhile, around the dining-room on the outside, uniformed policemen with Sten-guns and rifles were standing guard. A few plain-clothes men came as near to the dining-table as possible to eavesdrop on our conversation. They could easily do so, as the dining-room, like all the rooms in my house, had open louvred windows. My wife told me that while she was cooking, the plain-clothes men were talking among themselves loud enough, perhaps purposely, to let her overhear their conversation. Among other things one non-Malay D.P.C. was heard trying to convince his Malay colleague that it was conclusive that I must have got a lot of money from Indonesia; how else would I be able to build such a big house? No Malay could have such an amount of money, he added. My wife said she had been sorely tempted to give this Indian D.P.C. a piece of her mind, for so arbitrarily making such an accusation; but she thought better of it.

After that last meal in my home, I went upstairs with my wife, and both of us completed our evening prayer. At 7.40 p.m. I said to my captors, 'I am ready.' Only then did my wife break down. I consoled her by saying, 'It is a sure sign of want of Faith to cry and lose control of one's emotions. So trust in God, do what he commands, and live.' I told her that after a week had gone by she should make a request to visit me. A Malay Assistant Superintendent of Police (A.S.P.), who was in the party, also gave her this assurance.

Later my wife told me that Umi, my youngest child, aged nine, also broke down that evening, crying that now her father had been arrested, she supposed that she and her sister, Raziah, would have to leave school, as no one could support their schooling. I told my wife to submit to the Will of God, as Islam demands; she would then have peace and composure. To Raziah, my second youngest child, eleven years old and a student in Standard Five at the Batu Maung Sekolah Kebangsaan, and to her youngest sister, Umi Salamah, studying at the same school, in Standard Four, I said, 'Do not be afraid, as the Government cannot do anything to me such as beating me to death. Everything is in the hands of Allah; it is He who decided that I should be arrested. And do not neglect your religious studies or your school lessons.' After embracing my wife and both Raziah and Umi I left in the car, driven by Ah Chan. I sat next to him; Mr. Putra sat at the back. Waving good-bye, I felt calm and collected. My wife and the two children waved back to me without emotion. I felt very proud of them; they went on waving till I could see them no more. For them and for me—they were now only shadows against the lights of the house—I was going into darkness!

I sat in the car making small talk with my captors. We drove to Police Headquarters in Penang Road, stopping finally at the Special Branch entrance. Ah Chan looked around to see if there were any Press reporters about. We went up by lift to the Officers' Common Room. There I was told to wait, as another officer would be taking me to Kuala Lumpur. I was offered refreshments. At 8 p.m. I performed *Isha*, the last evening prayer.

II. JOURNEY

ABOUT 8.30 p.m. a Chinese Special Branch officer in a brand-new cream-coloured Volvo came to drive me to Kuala Lumpur, 250 miles away. He and I were accompanied by three D.S.P.s in plain clothes. They offered to pay the duty for the tobacco and other toilet requisites if demanded at the mainland Customs' barrier, Bagan Luar, where the car-ferry docked. The Customs Officer checking our car recognized me, and so did a Malay D.P.C. accompanying us. We were waved on—at least I was duty-free! Apart from the police, the Customs personnel at Bagan Luar must have been the first people to know that I had been arrested. The looks on their faces showed they suspected this, having read about the arrests of my associates in the Press that morning. Ever since I left the Alliance Government in February 1963 (I remained an M.P. until the end of the year when Parliament was dissolved), the Customs Officers in Penang, Johore Bahru and Singapore had always shown courtesy and kindness to me whenever I had occasion to come into contact with them in the course of their duties.

We drove on thirty-five miles to Bagan Serai where we stopped for a cup of coffee. The officer-in-charge was at the wheel; I sat next to him. He was a young man full of respect and consideration. At the coffee-shop I told him I wanted to go to the toilet, and so as not to make it too obvious I asked if any of them would go, too.

They would not allow me to pay for the coffee or a packet of cigarettes I bought. Clearly I was already the 'guest' of the Government. I would have liked to smoke my pipe, but conscious of the fact that the officer's car was new and the upholstery still smelt fresh, I feared the sparks from my tobacco might damage it. I told him so. He said that was thoughtful of me, and smiled.

At Tanjong Malim, 135 miles further on, we stopped again. There was no shop suitable for me to take my *Sahor*, the last meal before the dawn of a new day in Ramadan. We therefore drew up at a roadside day-and-night stall. I had some Milo with bread and margarine. It was 3 a.m. We arrived in Kuala Lumpur at the High Street Police Station at 4.20 a.m. One of the D.P.C.s had a flask of coffee, which he offered me. I still had a piece of chocolate which Umi, my youngest daughter, had given me before I left home. This I finally took before *Imsak*—the beginning of the fast immediately before dawn.

During the journey, although I was not my usual self, nevertheless I engaged the driver in small talk. I remember telling him jokingly that by the brand of car a police officer used I could determine his rank. 'At least,' I said, 'I can place an officer if his Volvo is a new one, or recently purchased. That means he has been recently promoted from the rank of an Inspector to one of gazetted rank, i.e., Assistant Superintendent.' An Inspector, I explained, would normally buy a Volkswagen, and usually sell it on being promoted to an A.S.P. This little observation of mine seemed to impress him; it certainly broke any ice between us. From then onwards I prattled away. Somehow I did not feel sleepy or tired; I was quite awake most of the time. Actually, my mind was rather a blank.

The officer-in-charge of my escort party went in to make a telephone call while I waited in his car together with the other three. It must have been more than forty minutes before a Black Maria arrived. I was grateful to the officer for not taking me into the Police Station, thus avoiding embarrassment for me. I had once seen a Black Maria before at a distance, but I also had read of it in detective stories. In fact, one story in my school-days told of some criminals being put into a Black Maria to be taken to gaol. I had also seen Black Marias in Kuala Lumpur near the Police Courts and Pudu Gaol. Prisoners going to gaol after court conviction were always taken in a Black Maria. In those days I had never suspected that I was ever going to be a passenger in one. I was introduced to a Malay police officer who came at the same time as the Black Maria. On being asked to get in I was ushered into a tiny compartment and asked to sit on a wooden bench, just sufficient for one person. The Maria had four such compartments. Quite apart from the colour of the vehicle, black, the inside of the compartment was completely dark. There was only a small hole right at the top, to serve as ventilator. It was so shaped that one could not see anything outside. Just sitting there for the first time, I felt suffocated!

The driver and another person in the Black Maria were in fact policemen. They were silent but respectful. Then we started on a journey, which reminded me of the old silent film, 'The Covered Wagon'. I felt just like that! The Maria travelled fast with sudden jerks and jolts, almost making me sick. The rough ride lasted about thirty minutes, but it seemed hours. On occasions I felt we were climbing a steep gradient, and then again we would be skirting a hair-pin corner. Sudden stops three times knocked my head against the walls of the compartment. The man at the wheel (I could not see him) drove like a maniac trying to catch a train. I had a feeling of extreme nausea. Silently I prayed, and then felt better.

At long last we arrived. There was a long wait. Then the Maria reversed furiously as if going up a steep hill. Just as suddenly it stopped. I must have looked in pretty bad shape when a torchlight fell on my face. The driver uttered an unemotional apology. He seemed friendly, but looked afraid. When I finally got out I could h ardly stand up straight. I wanted to vomit, but tried to prevent it, as it would be breaking my fast. In fact *Imsak* had not yet begun, but I did not know it then. However, I survived.

Officers then conducted me into what looked like the ground floor of a block of stone houses, walking past several locked rooms, until they came to an open one. There, a person I had known as a policeman some years ago asked me to remove my clothes to put on a kind of uniform. It was navy-blue, made of coarse cotton, fashioned like a pair of Chinese trousers. Reaching just below the knees, it had a shirt with short sleeves of the same colour and material, with a small pocket. Both pieces of clothing smelt of stale sweat, as if from an unclean body which had worn them unwashed for a long time. I was disgusted, but there was nothing I could do but put them on, at the same time trying not to show my distaste.

I pretended that this new life now forced upon me was one I was accustomed to. Keeping a cheerful face, I chatted with the Malay police officer about everything in general but nothing in particular. No responses at all; he listened to me silently. Then he, assisted by a Corporal and a Police Constable, all in mufti, started to draw up a list of all my belongings. They said I could take nothing with me. I even had to surrender my spectacles. At this request, I protested strongly, as I am near-sighted. If they insisted, I said I had no choice but to surrender them, but they would be responsible if I fell down and hurt myself as a result. Reluctantly, they agreed to let me keep them, but also hinted that the final decision about the glasses would rest with the Case Officer, who would see me later on. Later I realized that the Malay officer at the reception room had no powers, except to check me in; he had to abide strictly by the rules. All 'guests' were to be stripped of everything, even glasses. Anyone can imagine the physical discomfort, the strange and unusual feeling on having one's glasses taken away suddenly, after having become so accustomed to using them that they are a part of one's body. It was really terrifying! To become almost blind and completely lose your bearings. Ask yourself, would you like your 'eyes' removed? They did not even allow me to brush my teeth. Then they took me through a labyrinth of lanes among blocks of barracks, stopping from time to time at innumerable gates. At each of these my conductors had to get permission before proceeding any further. I had no idea at all where I was.

Finally they ushered me into a cell. I said I would like to say my *Suboh* prayer for the dawning of the new day. The policeman replied that he would have to ask permission first for me to take the *ud'uk* (ablution). Meanwhile he locked me in. About fifteen minutes later he took me out again, leading me to a bathroom for my ablutions. Then, after being locked in for a second time I performed the *Suboh* prayer. This is a simple, short verse that welcomes the new day, the call of the muezzin that runs with the rising of the sun around the whole Muslim world from minaret to minaret.

> Allah is Great! Allah is Great!
> There is no God but Allah
> And Mohamed is His Prophet!

As the first streaks of light rim the sky, the impressive simple chant of the prayer rolls out, echoing in the air. Not only a hymn to God, but the dawn of a new day He has given to men. A short prayer, only twelve lines, which ends eloquently with a reminder of duty and a gentle rebuke.

Come to Prayer! Come to Prayer!
Prayer is better than sleep!

It struck me forcibly then how very true it was, realizing this as if for the first time. Only twelve hours ago, I thought, I was peacefully reading the Koran in my room, in my own home. Since then my whole life had altered. I had not slept for twelve hours. I was not with those I love, but 250 miles away, alone, in prison, in a cell. And I could not, did not want to sleep. Yes, prayer is better than sleep! And so I prayed with all my heart—or I tried to.

III. FAITH

I am not ashamed to confess that the effect of the reception I received after my arrest the previous evening, the strange manner in which I was treated up to the moment I was put in a cell, had quite upset my equilibrium. Obviously this was what the Special Branch anticipated would happen to me. And it did.

Firstly, I was unable to achieve tranquillity in prayer. Had my Faith also been affected? If so, was it temporary? I realized that no man was perfect, least of all myself! But when a man tries to do his best in the service of God he is promised that his faults will be blotted out and he will be treated as if he had committed none at all. 'For God is yet forgiving and ready to appreciate service.' Only one with sincere, genuine repentance can hope for this blessing. My mind was still crowded with all the events of the few days before my detention. But my conscience was not disturbed; that I could honestly claim I was quite clean, whatever it might be I was accused of having committed.

Sleep was impossible. On that Friday morning in these strange surroundings, I did not for a moment think about myself. Foremost in my mind was worry for my father. He was seventy-six years old and had been discharged from hospital less than two weeks before, after being treated for a heart ailment. Equally disturbing was the fact that my eldest daughter was still a hospital patient, after three months of suffering from a chest disorder. I wondered if God would be kind to my father, at least to the extent that he would not be unduly worried about my arrest. This news might perhaps cause a relapse. Fervently I prayed for him, and likewise for my daughter, the type of girl who worries. If she should allow free rein to her emotions, and let herself worry, she would not be able to recover her health in the time expected. The physical condition of these two close relatives occupied almost

all my thoughts. Other members of my family seemed to fade
into the background. As to my own safety and well-being, I considered this of no importance, except for a lurking fear my fate
might be the same as that of Patrice Lumumba, murdered in
the Congo. I could not rule out the possibility of this happening;
there had been several attempts on my life when I was living at
Morib in Selangor.

Before moving to Batu Maung, I had lived there for eighteen
months, and during that time several attempts were made on my
life. The last attempt, and the most serious one, was by a group
of Chinese gangsters who tried several times to get access to my
compound, but failed. I had mentioned this incident in Parliament.
The Speaker, Datuk Haji Mohd. Noah bin Omar, asked me to
make a report at a Police Station. He granted me leave for an
hour, so I went to the High Street Police Station in Kuala Lumpur
to make a report. Subsequently the Assistant Commissioner of
Police, Encik Yusof bin Yunos, then Officer-in-charge of Anti-
Corruption, Federation of Malaya, received an assignment to
investigate the incident.

In any case, my worries and anxieties were only temporary,
for I remembered the well-known passage of *Sura Al-Baqara*:

> On no shoulder doth God
> Place a burden greater
> Than it can bear:
> It gets every good that it earns
> And it suffers every ill that it earns.

Somehow, as I said earlier, I did not seem able to attain complete
release from worry. Perhaps my Faith was not pure and unadul-
terated; that I know best myself! Anyhow it was a great comfort
and consolation to me now even to be able to remember this
great passage!

I could not sleep at all, not even during the day. In fact, I was
hoping to be able to get sufficient rest before the interrogation that
must inevitably come—when? So far I had not had a wink of sleep
since leaving Penang. I did not know what would happen. That
first day and night I will never forget. Anticipating that I would
be called for interrogation early, I was trying to think of what

to say. I imagined all manner of procedures, all kinds of questions—things I had read about in books, seen in films, or incidents related to me by people who had themselves been through the grill-mill before. Somehow, I was not afraid; in fact, quite confident. I had nothing to fear, except as a potential victim of murder. This thought kept prodding me. I knew that under present circumstances anything could happen to me, being very much aware of what human beings are capable of doing when their own well-being is threatened.

My cell had a cement floor; a raised slab of concrete served as my bed. It had a mattress of dirty, old khaki cloth full of holes; the filling was coconut fibre, which stuck out, pricking the skin all the time; it was no mattress at all. There was a blanket, too, but I do not remember it at that time. In the cell, there were mosquitoes everywhere, day and night. Twelve feet up, close to the ceiling, was a small hole—my only ventilation. Alas, the mosquitoes did not seem to know or care the hole was there; they stayed close to me, and actively! As far as I remember now, the cell measured about twelve feet by ten. From time to time a tiny aperture in the steel door would glide open, and someone would take a peep at me. I could see only his eyes. Whenever I looked at the peeping tom, the aperture would shut abruptly. I had no idea what time it was, but only knew when it was day because the cell became very hot with the rays of the sun beating on it. If I had a request to make, I had to bang hard on the steel door. After a moment someone would peep through the aperture, and ask what I wanted. I wanted a bath, I told the 'eyes'. A voice said he would let me know. Nothing happened.

Later, when I guessed it was time for the *Suhor* prayer, I banged on the steel door again, asking permission to go out for my ablution. After waiting about half an hour I was let out, and told to hurry up about it! I asked for some soap. It was not allowed, I was told. Tooth-brush? No! Towel? Also No! To every request—No! No! No! It seemed no one had any authority to grant me anything. After several polite requests, I surrendered, foregoing any wish to ask for anything any more. Those few young policemen who all said 'No', all of them seemed no more than twenty-three years of age; they were polite, but very neutral. I washed myself as best as I could with water in the bathroom-cum-lavatory. While doing so, I realized for the first time that one of the methods adopted for detainees was to demoralize them completely by design before arraigning them for interrogation. Obviously from my present experience this was normal practice. I could not believe it could really be true. I had not even been charged yet, so why this treatment? Why?

IV. INTERROGATION

SLOWLY it began to dawn upon me what true values were. Ordinary things like freedom of movement and such common everyday necessities as soap, a towel, a tooth-brush, etc. were denied to me. One is so used to such things as part of the daily routine of living, that one has no occasion to question any need for them. I concluded, therefore, that denial of these simple articles was one of the psychological weapons adopted by Government to coerce detainees into confession—that is, if they were not made of sterner stuff.

Perhaps I should not continue to divulge any more of the kind of life I was forced to live in that unknown detention camp before and during the time statements were to be extracted from me. I am fully conscious of the fact that the methods used are those inherited from the British. Since these are the only methods known to us in Malaysia, whatever Government may come into power in future, and if the Internal Security Act continues, it is probably best for me not to reveal too much of the actual ways of extracting confessions from detainees. I would like to say, however, that essentially this centre where my interrogations took place was meant for Communists, and not Nationalists like me. Up to this time, no Nationalist had ever been detained there before. In the days of Colonial rule no thought had ever been given to building a detention camp for fair and humane treatment of political prisoners. Therefore, the centre where I was kept was meant for Communists, built in 1951–2, and, of course, no Malay had ever been an inmate. And certainly no former Minister!

In my time as a journalist I had been closely associated with the Police Force. In fact there were not many officers from the rank and file right up to the Commissioner himself, or the Inspector-General, who were not known to me. This fact must have been taken into consideration by the authorities when they assigned the officers to interrogate me. This was true. They had made a slip in the case of Ah Chan who led the party to arrest me at my home. They did not anticipate that I knew him, but I did. As to the officers who were to be my interrogators, all three were unknown to me personally. What criteria were adopted and what special merits these officers possessed to be selected in my case were factors that must have taken the Special Branch V.I.P.s some considerable time and thought to decide. But one qualification these officers must have in common would be—no respect for me as a former Minister of Government. They were to treat me strictly as a detainee. I know that one of them actually relished his assignment. I will say no more about him, lest I reveal his identity.

The next evening—twelve hours after I had entered the cell—a policeman led me out. He put me in handcuffs and escorted me through a maze of passages, ultimately arriving at the interrogation room. There, after asking me to sit down, the Chief Interrogator instructed the policeman to remove my handcuffs. When the first interrogation was over I was handcuffed again. This same procedure occurred on each of four or five days, until perhaps they began to realise that I had nothing to hide when I gave my answers to their hundreds of questions.

On being led into the interrogation room the first time, I was being my natural self. The room was medium-sized, about sixteen feet square. There was a fan. The table was near a window with a chair in front and three behind. A naked light blazed quite strongly. The bulb must have been at least 100 watts. The Chief Interrogator, a Malay about thirty-two years old, sat with his back towards the half-opened window. On his right sat an Indian Police Inspector; he was in fact a Chief Police Inspector; on his left a young Malay Inspector of Police. He looked Chinese but actually he was Malay. When I came in they were all seated. I greeted them, but none responded. They pretended to look stern. They asked me to sit in front of the table.

I asked, 'Can I be introduced?' This request seemed to upset all three; they had not expected this to happen.

I remarked, 'How can I stay and be with you for the next few

days without even knowing who you are or what to call you.'
Very reluctantly they conceded, although the leader murmured,
'It is not necessary to know our names.'

I began to wonder if I were in their place, and they in mine,
would they have acted as I did? I believed not. They would be
terrified. I was anything but afraid of them. This again was Faith.
When they tried to talk to me toughly, I said I was not used to
any rough manners they might adopt.

'Tell your story truthfully,' I was told.

At one stage, the leader said, 'You are a detainee, and as such
have no rights whatsoever.'

Eventually we came to an understanding that no rough tactics
would be adopted throughout the interrogation. They were, of
course, service officers doing a job of work; but to what degree
they exceeded their normal duties would be very obvious to me.
After all, at my age, knowing human nature, especially among
our own people, officers like these can easily be classified—the
truly efficient, the time-servers, the sycophants and others. I was
to be associated with these three for over a month, so during that
period I can now confidently say that I soon came to know them
very well indeed.

The first session lasted more than two hours before darkness
set in. Subsequent sessions started after dinner, or after the *Isha*
prayer, and lasted for two or three hours, until about ten or eleven
p.m. During one night session I asked to be allowed to smoke
my pipe with my own tobacco, which they had retained. They
refused flatly, but they themselves smoked. In so doing perhaps
they intended mentally to torture me. Only when they thought
that I had opened up a little would they offer me a cigarette or
two. But when I told them that it was my habit to smoke in the
morning before moving my bowels, they instructed a guard to
present me with a single cigarette in the early morning.

The Prophet's close friend, Sayidana Ali, used to categorize
human beings into three types, if anyone can truly claim to know
other people at all. They are—those who have lived together;
those who have done business together; and those who have gone
on a long journey together. In my case I endured the business
and skullduggery of these Special Branch officers for more than

a month, and came to know very well the parries and thrusts of their game. I flatter myself, therefore, in being able to evaluate their true worth, both as officers and as human beings.

More than once my Case Officers asked me, apropos of nothing in particular, if I knew the location of the centre where I was being held. I said I did not. In fact the location of this place, known as the Holding Centre, was a jealously-guarded secret. For more reasons than one it had to be. The security of the place itself, especially the identities of the inmates, should not be known to anyone, even to those working in the Police Force—in fact, to no one, that is, other than the Special Branch officers assigned directly to such duties. I remember very well that once I was invited to visit this Centre when I was a Minister. In fact, I had been asked several times to go there, but I had not done so. All my other colleagues, without exception, had visited the place, and were shown how the Centre worked. Actually the British Government was rather proud of the place. Douglas Hyde, the anti-Communist expert, an ex-Communist himself, had had a hand in the actual organizing and planning of the methods of coercion and persuasion into submission of the inmates in this Centre. But the fundamental approach and the system of extracting information were originally based on Scotland Yard methods, not counting, of course, Asian impatience and irresponsibility on top of it all.

Perhaps if I had visited the place during my time in office as a Minister I would not have been taken to the Centre at all. I would be too *au fait* with the closely-guarded secret methods of interrogation. I was told the British were jealous of their methods, and unwilling to allow even the F.B.I. to know about them.

Anyway, I do know that each officer in the Police Force there had to pledge to keep secret the location of the place and the goings-on there. In the course of their duties they were not to converse with the inmates, nor were they to divulge their own names. As a result of these rules, they became themselves automatons.

V. BREAKING BARRIERS

MOST of the uniformed policemen at the Centre were young. Many were English-educated. I knew that a few had either taken the School Certificate Examination, or were about to do so. Later I found out the penalty of breaking their bond to the Special Branch was a $2,000 fine, and/or two years in prison, or both. I do not wonder, therefore, that these policemen lived in continuous fear lest they should ever slip up. Their nightmare behaviour on my first day at the Centre now became clear to me. Those first few days with these young Malay policemen were rather like associating with inanimate objects. They herded the detainees around, sometimes in handcuffs, sometimes without, but always impersonally. Only some would volunteer a hesitant smile. No one could think of or expect any sympathy from them, but of the number we met daily, only a few seemed quite unfriendly. With these, even time did not seem to break any barrier. I, however, told these unfriendly young policemen that in our sorry plight, the anxiety and suffering we had in our cells, it would be of great cheer to us if they would smile a little. To us, a slight smile could mean consolation. 'None of you,' I said, 'should appoint yourself a judge of what we are alleged to have committed. Only God has the full facts of the case, not even the Special Branch; and the Special Branch is not free from making mistakes.' Nevertheless, they were human beings: that was fundamental. During the later stages of my detention, in the quiet of the night I could often overhear their conversations on every subject under the sun. They were, of course, under the impression that we were asleep or that we had lost interest in mundane affairs.

I was detained at the Federal Holding Centre for nearly three months. During this period I came across, more or less, some thirty or forty policemen on guard duties there. Of the number of young Malay policemen, I observed particularly that only three out of about thirty regularly performed the five daily prayers. Perhaps a few did not want to be too obvious about prayers, preferring to perform them when they got back to their quarters. But this possibility was remote.

Before my internment, for nearly two years I had made a special study of our own people, the Malays, in the field of religion. These observations I carried out in Selangor, Johore and Penang. I met several teachers from religious schools, Imams and kampung elders, and recorded their observations and experiences of the true position of the Faith among the kampung people, who by tradition had inherited from their own forefathers at least six or seven centuries of Islam.

Kampung society, according to many observers, has deteriorated in the past fifty years. The speed of deterioration accelerated in the past thirty years, reaching its peak after World War II. Kampung religious leaders informed me that thirty years ago there was no need to coerce kampung people to go to the *Surau* or the Mosque. Friday prayers would always fill the Mosque to capacity. Now in many kampungs even the minimum to make a congregation legal, that is forty devotees present, is sometimes not available, so Friday prayers have to be reduced to an ordinary *Zuhur* prayer. *Zuhur* is the prayer when the day turns to afternoon. I also found that the average of regular performers of *Waktu* (the five times of prayer) among kampung dwellers or Government servants or general wage-earners was the same—about 10% of the total, either for those living in the towns or in the kampungs.

I am not, of course, deviating from my theme; rather I am trying to convey how my mind was working about three years before I was detained. How during that period I was trying to analyse roughly the worth of religious knowledge and the piety of an ordinary Malay. While I was languishing in my detention, naturally my thoughts continued to run on this evaluation. As we always had time on our hands to think, it is a bitter truth to realize how superficially our people have in the past generations taken up religion. When I posed this question, more than one Imam admitted it was a fact. How many of his congregation in performing a prayer knows exactly the words in his own language of the prayer itself? What percentage? Invariably I found that the Imam, faced for the first time in his life with such a question, would be very shocked. Willy-nilly he had to admit that not more than 10% of those performing the five regular daily prayers were conversant with the Malay meaning of the words of the prayers. In other words, if in a kampung 100 attend the Friday prayers only ten perform the five daily prayers, and out of this small number only one understands the meaning of the prayers he utters in Arabic. Such is the state of religious progress among our own people today.

During the early period of my detention at the Federal Holding Centre several Special Branch officers used to visit me. This was during the second month of my stay; before that no one visited me in my cell. Some Malay Special Branch officers used to take an interest in what I did, and their curiosity included what I was reading or writing. The interest shown by some officers was not entirely professional. There were some genuine Malay Nationalists even among them, but they were unable to show or disclose their political leanings at the risk of losing their jobs. Some showed their kindness in trying to make me as comfortable as possible without at the same time doing it obviously. At that time, and even now, I still cannot fathom the intentions of these officers. It is very wrong to label all Special Branch officers as being devoid of human feelings, but he must be a simpleton indeed if he trusts them out-of-hand after what I experienced of their performances. Some officers even looked at passages of the translation of the Koran I was studying, and were genuinely surprised that at my age, fifty years old, I was starting all over again. I told them how in my early youth I, like any ordinary young Malay, made a study of elementary religious knowledge, such as *Rukun Iman* (The Principle of Faith), and *Rukun Islam* (The Pillars of Islam). And that I used to pray quite earnestly when I was young. Since I began working, my religious progress had been almost nil. In fact, I continued to deteriorate in the society of English-educated Malays to which I belonged, going only occasionally to the mosque on Fridays. Fasting during the month of Ramadan I seldom missed, but its true significance did not make much impression on my mind. Sometimes when I was in trouble I would start to pray, but when the trouble was over my praying stopped, too. I went on like this for many years.

I related the history of my religious downfall to those officers who interrogated me. I was happy to note that it was not wasted on them. The leader of one group, realizing that he was an English-educated Malay like me, and had also neglected the religious side of his own children's education, actually told me he would endeavour to rectify his ways. Another Malay officer challenged me, saying, 'There is no such thing as God's mercy. If there is, God certainly will not make a criminal of anyone so he can commit murder.'

'I am not prepared to argue with anyone who has no religious background at all,' I said. 'We will only be wasting our time, arguing in circles and getting nowhere. One can only discuss it with someone whose religious knowledge is of about an equal standard, or whose piety is much the same.'

Anyway, I explained to him and to others present that a person became bad and committed crimes because he was forgetful of God; in fact, his remembrance of God was nil, or almost nil. I related the story of the Creation of Man as taken from the Koran. When God announced to the angels that He was about to create man, Iblis objected. Iblis said all the angels including himself were superior to man, God's new creation, and therefore it would be undignified for them to honour a being made of sounding clay when they themselves were created from something pure, that is, fire. God was angry with Iblis and condemned him to Hell.

Iblis, however, asked for a respite during the existence of this world in order to harass and thus influence man to follow the ways of Evil. God granted Iblis this request, saying that no amount of harassment, persuasion or influence could make those whose faith in God was deep-rooted follow the path of evil; only those whose faith was shaky would fall to the wiles of Iblis.

'Therefore,' I said, 'those who commit crimes of murder, robbery or swindling, etc. are in the category of those having no faith in God, and so God does not extend His bounty or mercy to them. But, of course, the most hardened criminal can receive God's bounty and mercy again if he repents and changes his former ways of life and does not forget to remember God.'

I think this explanation of mine rather impressed the Special Branch officers present. Except for one or two, the rest had never heard of this quite familiar piece in the Koran I had with me. They told me that they would themselves buy a copy and would without delay start to follow my example. One officer, however, confessed that in his youth he studied religion at a *pondok* in Trengganu before the war and had quite a sound religious background, but, like most English-educated Malays, he had not found time to perform his five daily prayers. He then declared he would rectify this. Observing me at my age, he said I had restarted almost from scratch on my new endeavour, and he wished me well. Another officer, who asked me many questions on the subject of prayer, said he was afraid to recommence praying as he had neglected doing so entirely for many years. And he had been told it was illegal for him to start again if he had not completed praying for the whole period of years that he had missed performing his prayers. I told him that I was also a new student, but it was quite misleading for anyone to have to pay in full the number of prayers he had missed, performing five times a day for so many years past. It must amount to several thousand. What we should do is merely to begin again, after complete repentance for past mistakes, by performing the five daily rituals and supplementing them by performing the *Sunat* before or after compulsory prayers accordingly. He seemed grateful for this, especially when I said that my teacher had told me this was the right procedure.

Another officer, however, was very sceptical. While admitting the great value of the translation of the Koran I was studying, he tried to belittle my efforts. 'You are not genuinely interested in religion,' he remarked, 'you are merely trying to impress me as a Special Branch officer and so give me a false impression of your worth.'

Later on, when I had occasion to meet this same officer several times at another place during my detention, he must have realized that although I was a beginner in religion, I was at least keen and in earnest. I was not a fraud. Subsequently when I referred to several passages from the Koran when discussing my detention, he would say that he also had many relatives who were quite *au fait* with religion. They had been to Mecca, too, and were able to quote passages from the Koran as well. This officer was formerly an English school-master who later joined the Police Force. It was clear to me that he, lacking merit in his work, wanted to make up by exceeding his normal responsibilities so as to gain promotion.

So during the long days of my detention I had the satisfaction—looking back I can truthfully call it such—not only of interesting my own warders in religion, but in doing so breaking down the barriers of their automatism and bringing them to realize that all of us, detainer or detained, are just human beings, and all equal in the eyes of God, like all people in the world.

VI. HOME FRONT

DURING my first month of detention, not for one moment did I worry about how my family was facing the day-to-day essentials of making ends meet at home. There was no point in doing so; I was sure they would find ways to cope. I did not see any of them until three weeks after my detention. There was no Hari Raya Festival for any of us that year.

I thought it rather strange that, although I was aware that the families of other detainees visited their relatives one week after, or within a week of their being detained, I was denied this privilege. Later on, after my release, I found out why. After about a week in detention I asked my Case Officer whether I could see my family. In a rather typical reply, designed to discourage and to delay any action, he told me that my request could not be entertained. He further tried to explain in a round-about-way that it had never happened before; no request had ever come from a detainee. He even hinted at the possibility that my family did not want to see me.

'There is no precedent for a detainee himself to make a request to see his family,' he said.

'I would like to break the precedent,' I replied.

Then he stated that my request would be forwarded to his senior officer. At the same time, he informed me that Dr. Tan Chee Khoon, the Socialist Front M.P., would like to see me, and also that Mr. K.L. Devaser, my lawyer, wished to visit me.

'I want top priority to see my family before seeing anyone else,' I said. He answered, 'If you see anyone within one week, you cannot see any other person for another week.'

In fact it was already clear to me that their tactics were to get me to clear up my statements first, before I would be allowed to see anyone lest my mental condition, which they had been working up to a high pitch, would become normal again, and then I would revert to a state of disillusionment. Perhaps this is what they wanted to happen! In the end, they did fix a date for me to see my family for the first time. I was allowed to shave, and have my hair cut. Naturally I was looking forward keenly to seeing my wife and children. But it was not to be. The day fixed for the meeting with my family in Kuala Lumpur turned out to be a day of riots. What the riot was all about I did not know at that time, and did not learn of it until two days later. According to the *Sunday Times* of 14 February 1965 'more than 1,500 slogan-chanting youths ran riot' in Kuala Lumpur on Saturday 13 February. They were protesting against 'the Government's ban on a rally the Socialist Front wanted to hold to condemn the arrest of its leaders'.

Apparently the rioters had congregated at five different points, armed with spears, parangs, knives, broken bottles and bicycle chains. The riot lasted three hours, from 9 a.m. to noon, before the police restored calm. They also imposed a curfew in the centre of the town that night. Outside this area everything was normal. Altogether 100 rioters were arrested, as well as three Socialist Front leaders taken at their own Headquarters including the Chairman, the Secretary-General, the Assistant Secretary and the Vice-President of the Labour Party. All were detained under the Internal Security Act. Although a lot of damage was done to shop-windows, no one was hurt. A Government spokesman said the disturbances were definitely Communist-inspired and could be linked with landings by Indonesian troops at Kukup Island the day before.

I learned later that the riot also had repercussions in Penang; Special Branch officers called to see my wife in Batu Maung the day before the riot. They came to ask if she was the leader of a local group planning to leave for Kuala Lumpur that day. My wife knew nothing of the affair and said so. Later she learned that four busloads of people in Batu Maung had intended to go to the capital to demonstrate against the arrest of Opposition leaders, including me.

According to the *Sunday Times* the day after the riot, 'More than 500 members of the Socialist Front in Penang had planned to come down to Kuala Lumpur in chartered buses but were stopped by the police. One bus with thirty-five people aboard, however, got through the police line.' The police had also picked up some people from Penang, who had tried to reach Kuala Lumpur by train. They were stopped at Tanjong Malim station, fifty miles north of the capital.

I found out much later that would-be demonstrators from Penang had been told to go on their own by any means possible. The people of Batu Maung, being unprepared, could not make the necessary arrangements in time. Except for a few, the rest abandoned the trip. Although many of the village women visited my wife in our home, she had never been told of any plan to hold a mammoth demonstration in Kuala Lumpur. In fact, when asked by the Head of Special Branch, Penang, if she was going to Kuala Lumpur, she innocently said she was; she was going by bus to see me. He told her, however, not to go by bus. He meant, of course, any of the buses in which the demonstrators from Penang had booked to go. But my wife wanted to go to Kuala Lumpur by the Express Bus Service, which leaves Bagan Luar every morning at 9 a.m. arriving in Kuala Lumpur at about 5 p.m. the same day—a normal service. She would have preferred to go by train, as she was used to travelling first-class since 1951 when I first became a Member of the Federal Legislative Council, and as such entitled to complimentary railway passes. As I was not re-elected in 1964, we no longer had such passes. Very wisely she decided, both as a money-saver as well as a face-saver, that she would rather travel in a non-class express bus to and from Kuala Lumpur to visit me in detention. A single fare cost only $12.

Since I had to sell my car to pay my 1962 income tax commitments, just before my detention, I was without any means of personal transport. For my three children and my wife each trip to Kuala Lumpur would cost her $96/- to and from the capital. This sum with incidental expenses would total not less than $120/- each time they visited me. Actually, she was only able to visit me twelve times altogether, although she was entitled to see me once a week. Therefore, she must have spent a total of not less than $1,500 during my detention, money she got from friends and near relations.

On one occasion, I suggested to a Senior officer of Special Branch that the least the Government could do was to provide free transport for my wife and children to visit me in Kuala Lumpur. I believe my proposal was never taken seriously.

Exactly twenty-five days after my initial detention my wife and all my children came to see me—the whole family together again, briefly. Previously, however, my son, Zakaria, had seen me at the High Street Police Station. He brought me some cakes from Penang for the Hari Raya Festival—now alas long since past. This happened about two weeks after my detention, being one result of my strong protests that normal red-tape should be abandoned so that any requests of mine to see my family should be agreed to, rather than requests having to come from them. During the first meeting with my son at the High Street Police Station, my Case Officer was present personally, so our conversation, of course, could not be other than disjointed enquiries about the well-being of various members of the family. I could not tell my son anything about the conditions under which I was being held. Naturally I tried to make him feel that I was quite comfortable (which was at that time far from the truth). As I could sense that my family, including my father, had all been unduly worried since my arrest, I asked Zakaria to reassure everyone that I was not being badly treated or beaten up. I could see that he was taking my reassurances with a pinch of salt.

In these modern times, the themes of books and films often portray most detailed methods of treating political prisoners, including beatings-up, or third-degree torture, or how interrogations are conducted and confessions extracted. The history of my own persecution ever since I fell from grace with my former colleagues was quite well-known to all members of my own family. Several attempts to do me bodily harm were revealed publicly. All these past tribulations naturally added to their extreme anxiety and fears for my well-being and safety now. My own feelings were detached, stoical, calm. I turned my son's attention to some passages of the Koran, such as, 'But God Knoweth best, those who do wrong', and God directs one's thoughts to 'Follow the inspiration sent to us, and to be patient and constant till He decides, for He is the best to decide'.

The Special Branch officer present on one such occasion intervened in our conversation enquiring about the identity of some

persons being referred to in our talks. Special Branch does not
speak all languages. Families have their own!

I must mention here the kindness of the leader of my interrogators, who brought me some cakes at Hari Raya. However, I was
not allowed to take them back to my cell; they had to be kept
at the guard post. Unfortunately, next day when I asked for them,
I found, after allowing for those I had eaten the previous day,
that the gift was greatly diminished in size and number.

My wife and family first came to see me exactly twenty-five
days after my arrest. Overwhelmed with happiness and emotion
at seeing all of them together, I was not at all sure how to begin
my conversation. But my wife solved this difficulty. She greeted
me by saying, 'Our revered ancestor's forecast has come to pass.'
Obviously she was referring to the riot. She was neither discouraged nor dampened in spirits when she mentioned this. I for
my part felt quite unmoved, as the matter she referred to was
something from which I had completely dissociated myself more
than two years before my detention.

Now, for the sake of giving an insight into my earlier spiritual
misconceptions I relate this story for what it is worth. Take it
as if one was reading a newspaper—half of its contents untrue, the
other half a half-truth! More than three years previously, to be
exact in the early part of 1962, I had a dream one night. It was a
complete dream, very clear and straightforward. I dreamed that an
ancestor of mine, who revealed himself as a great saint and ruler
in Sumatra around 700 years ago, said that the time was near when
a revolution would take place in Malaya. It would be a religious
revolution, or a revolution which would result in the religious
reformation for all people who followed Islam. My ancestor-saint
had quoted the Koran:

> Help from God
> And a speedy victory.
> So give the Glad Tidings
> To the Believers.
>
> No vision can grasp Him
> But His grasp is over
> All vision: He is

Above all comprehension
Yet is acquainted with all things.

And (the Unbelievers) plotted and planned,
And God too planned,
And the best of planners
Is God.

VII. THE DREAM

MY constant and continuous interest in the religious well-being of our people might have been the cause of this dream. Man, pursuing diverse aims, may find that owing to his own position, God's light is hidden from him now and then. In my own case it happens from time to time. But one must strive hard, indeed very hard, to turn towards and to reach this light—in all its glory. Without striving and determination this cannot be achieved. In the very nature and aims of men there are wide contrasts between their will for good or for evil. Therefore, evil may for a time obscure the good in man, but it cannot blot it out entirely, as, however evil a person may be, there is always some good in him. So, to achieve good for all time, man must seek out the highest truth, that is, only from the light of God. As to our people in Malaysia, and perhaps in most Muslim countries, the saying that, but for the elders who continue to seek the highest truth and the young innocents who have not yet accumulated worldly sins, perdition would have blotted out the earth as we know it, this may well be so.

There are many examples in the Koran—the Great Flood of Prophet Noah, or the fate of Thamud where the rich oppressed the poor, resulting in the complete extermination of its people when the Prophet Saleh failed to reform them. In the time of the Prophet Shuaib an earthquake buried a city and its people who had continued to practise fraud and commercial crimes. The Prophet Lot failed to change the habits of all those inclined to crimes against nature, those who died by fire in Sodom and Gomorrah. As another example, there is the annihilation by drowning of the Pharaoh and all his army in the era of Moses. Individuals, races, nations—yes, the whole world itself—can be exterminated if people neglect or refuse to accept God's light and His blessings.

Evil shows itself in various forms such as (i) Selfish greed and denial of other people's rights, (ii) Arrogance and attitudes of self-pride (such a man looks upon himself as self-sufficient, thus taking for his own the gifts of God), and (iii) Knowingly dishonouring truth through spite, or seeing ugliness where there is beauty. With such men or races the decline of a nation downward gathers momentum as they continue to go with their evil ways; their final fate can be nothing but misery. In the end, where will be their boasted wealth, their possessions or their self-conceit? The story of the Thamud and the Prophet Saleh belong to Arabian tradition. It took place in the north-west corner of Arabia between Medina and Syria. The story of the Prophet Shuaib also belongs to Arab rather than to Jewish tradition to which he is unknown. He lived in the fourth generation from the Prophet Abraham.

Well do I remember a song some years ago, 'Money is the Root of all Evil'. No title can be nearer to truth. Greed for wealth is and has been a root evil of the ills of the world ever since the Creation. I am glad that ever since I lost money in a fishing business in Singapore before I came to Malaya in 1948, I decided to forget that experience and forgo any desire to acquire money just for the sake of being rich. If money comes my way legally, well and good, but I refuse absolutely to seek out money. For me this has been a guiding principle for the past twenty-five years. In a broader sense wealth must be understood not only as money or material goods, but also as any advantage or opportunity a man happens to enjoy, which he can place at the service of others. As interpreted by a God-fearing man, wealth is not for selfish enjoyment or idle show, as can be observed everywhere around us today. In fact, to a good Muslim, wealth is a gift to be held in trust. The ownership of wealth can bring much tribulation in its train, but a true Muslim who uses it well can overcome any trial and even emerge purer in his life. His proper use of wealth increases his esteem and dignity, morally and spiritually. Such a man is a rare bird, but occasionally one does come across people with such qualities, or more often hears about them from others!

Briefly then, this was the basis of my dream, that there would soon be a religious revolution in our own country. How soon in our reckoning of time is anyone's guess—only God knows! Perhaps in our own life-time. At least, I hope and pray that it will come about while I am alive. For me, life really began from the night of this very significant dream. I pondered deeply and long on its meaning, and decided to abandon my past way of life, and to abjure all those things which Islam forbids. I endeavoured to do this to the best of my ability with God's guidance. How far I have succeeded only God and myself know. No other human being is qualified to judge.

The second part of the dream was the one my wife referred to—my arrest and detention—this came to pass. Followed by rioting—this also came to pass. The final episode of the dream has yet to come. The Government will change, and evil-doers will be identified. God's Will and His plans work out in their own good time. All ships on the ocean leave a wash behind them. So it was with this dream; the wash was my deep self-analysis in relation to the spiritual world. For many hundreds of years my ancestors were born Muslims. A Malay Muslim is very sensitive about religion. If he should be accused of being anything but a Muslim, he might even kill. But in actual fact questions arise—how much of him is truly Islamic? How deep is his religion? These questions can be answered. It strikes me that my own conversion from a non-practising Muslim to one who rigidly observes the dictates of Islamic law is significant.

I recall that during the rare occasions I attended the Friday prayers I often heard the *Khutbah* or sermon, read by the *Khatib*, the person chosen to deliver it. The significance of such oft-repeated phrases such as '*Ya ayuhan nas*' and '*Ya ayuhallazi-na ama nu*' had never been brought home to me. I half-knew the meaning of both, but until the dream, I had not tried to analyse them. Now I began to ask myself what the *Khatib* intends when addressing the congregation if he mentions the Koranic passage '*Ya ayuhan nas*'—meaning, 'O ye men,' or 'O ye Human beings'. Clearly it meant all of us, including me. But if the passage '*Ya ayuhallazi-na ama nu*' is mentioned, does it also cover all of us, including me? By right it should, because in English it is 'O ye who have Faith,' meaning 'O ye of the Muslim Faith.'

Now I began to ask myself again if this included me. Straight-away I had to admit it did not. Although I claimed to profess the Muslim Faith, I was not a practising Muslim. I went to the *Ju-ma'at* prayers only when I pleased. I think it was in 1936 when I last prayed regularly, five times a day, continuously. That was just after I was first appointed Fisheries Officer, Negeri Sembilan and Pahang. To have to admit this truth to myself was rather soul-searing. However, I am not ashamed to confess that, like the greater number of those who pray, I was in the same category as the 99% who utter prayers without knowing the meaning of what they say. In fact, worse; some passages of the Koran I had to re-learn; I had wholly forgotten them. But at that time, I was rather shy about asking anyone for guidance. I plodded along on my own, closely observing the various congregations in the mosques when *Sunat* (additional, voluntary) prayers were offered. And I made use of my old books, spending much time over them. After a while I no longer felt shy; in fact I felt quite confident with all the rituals. Later on I found a book called *Senjata To Haji dan Lebai*, which gives much useful guidance for those who aspire to be kampung elders. It means 'The Weapons for a Haji and Those Religiously-inclined'.

In my case, not having performed the pilgrimage to Mecca, the Haj, but only the Umrah, a minor form of the Haj, done out of proper season, I suppose I can qualify to be known as To' Lebai. But I don't aspire even to this honorific title. I am thinking of the adage that practice makes perfect. This always applies whe-ther to rituals in prayer, or even to golf. I went on trying with all the confidence I could muster, sometimes with none at all, until from time to time I was able to feel that I was making real progress—*Alhamdullilah* ('Praise be to God!')—and so I was amply rewarded for my efforts. If I was a typical example of a Malay not practising the dictates of Islam, what was I really? Clearly I was not a Muslim! It was quite a shock to have to realize this, to admit it. But still true! So it is also with those 90% of the total of non-practising Malays who inherit the Muslim religion from their fathers but do not perform prayers regularly.

Therefore, foremost in my mind now is a desire to take part in a programme to convert to practising Muslims Malays who hitherto have not carried out their regular prayers, following the dictates of Islam. How this is to be done is a supreme problem. I am sure I am right about one aspect—the manner of approach. This should always be such as not to antagonize anyone in the process of conversion. Use the velvet glove with the utmost tact, appealing to what they are not, rather than to what they are or should be. In my view, a brains-trust should first be set up to work on the correct manner of approach. Religious men dedicated to such work should come together, men of God, men who have the confidence of the masses. One *Ustaz* (that is, a progressive type of man) told me my plan should be successful if the right approaches were made by categories. For those who have the true desire, the right urge to reform, the tactful, velvet-glove method should suffice. But for more hardened types, those to whom the light of God has not yet penetrated at all, an entirely different approach would be needed. Then there are children, and also those just nearing puberty; these would need to be treated in still another way.

I agree completely. In fact, I have tried with some of my own children, and the results, I find, are most interesting, if not rewarding. Hence, it is necessary to choose such a brains-trust wisely. All should work in the name of Allah—nothing more and nothing less. They should expect no reward of money or in kind; they should ask only for the Mercy of God.

This idea of reform in Islam occupied my mind during the whole period of my detention. The objective is sincere and honest. If one is to take part, the process of self-improvement and self-cleansing must first be achieved, if such valuable work is to be recognized. The character and background of any workers on this kind of mission should be above question; only genuine servants of God are good enough. I realized then, and do so still, that the task will not be easy. Opposition will be strong in many quarters, particularly from old-fashioned religious teachers in the kampungs. The yes-men among the *Ulamas*, those learned in Islamic Law, could be a power to reckon with. British and American influences in Malaysia would also be strong opponents. They would be among the first to recognize a potential threat to their influence. In fact, to the Western Powers generally, any threat to their influence in either the politics or economics of any country, either directly or through religion, is a threat indeed.

I mentioned this particular idea of mine to a senior Special Branch officer whose religious background is well-known, but I don't believe he understood me correctly. He was thinking of my participating in the Muballigh, the Muslim Missionary Society, now functioning in Kuala Lumpur. Nothing was further away from my thoughts.

There are, I know, quite a number of people in Malaysia who, like me, are anxious to do something in this field of religious re-education of our people, but they have not had the time to give thought to their intentions. These good people will form the nucleus of the new Muslim brains-trust I was dreaming about. So my mind ran on and away each day and night—the loneliness of a cell gives one plenty of time for serious thought. In fact, it is the only way to live in solitude. I feel deeply sorry for those who are condemned to solitary confinement and are not able to think, not able to use the mind God has given each man. For such men there can only be decline—growing depression, sinking ever deeper into melancholia, and finally, despair.

VIII. ORDER OF DETENTION

ABOUT a week after my interrogation began—I had already had twelve sessions with my Case Officers—the guards moved me to another cell, which I call Number 2. This new cell was about the same size as the first. Of course there was a slight difference—more natural light from the ventilation at the top, fewer plaguey mosquitoes, but the light bulb was twice as bright, perhaps 200 kw. This naked bulb was alight day and night. A little morning sun seeped through the ventilation hole of the cell, but the full impact of the setting sun heated the wall. The cell was at the end of a long row. Because of this, after 4 p.m. each day the cell was a hot oven. This oven of mine did not grow any cooler until the small hours of the morning. So sleep was not easy to come by, and throughout each night I was dripping with sweat. My bedstead was a rickety plank, covered by a discoloured khaki cloth, which smelled strongly of stale sweat. Apparently, it had never been washed since it was first purchased. There was no linen of any kind. The only redeeming feature of this covering was—it was not torn. Nor was there any coconut fibre stuffing to irritate my back.

Interrogations continued every day, sometimes twice a day. The routine was always the same—suddenly without warning a guard opens the door, I go out of my oven, walk to the 'grill-room, meet my interrogators, and the questions and answers begin, and go on and on. Altogether during my stay in Cells Nos. 1 and 2, I was interrogated almost forty times, the shortest session being an hour, the longer ones two or two-and-a-half. The periods varied, sometimes in the morning, perhaps the evening or at night, but not after midnight. I never knew when I would be called. At first these sudden summons were very depressing, but later they became quite routine to me. Oddly enough, I was not at all surprised

when I first found myself in No. 2. Obviously from my interrogators' point of view progress was being made. I, however, did
not think they were making any progress at all, because, after
all, what had I done to make any progress about?

One day while I was in Cell No. 2 my Chief Case Officer—
or the Interrogator—asked me how I liked my new cell. I replied,
'I am not too lonely, as I am not alone.' He looked shocked; perhaps
he did not hear me properly. I repeated that I was not alone. I
recalled that the Holy Prophet with his companion Sayidina Abu
Bakar had taken shelter in a cave at Hiraa when he was being
hunted by the pagan Quraish. Abu Bakar remarked that they were
alone in the cave. The Prophet disagreed, saying, 'God is together
with us.' My reference to this episode from the Prophet's life
startled my interrogator. For once, he was at a loss for words.

During confinement in my first and second cells, detainees did
not see each other, I could hear only their voices, when going
to the toilet or for a drink in the bathroom. Repeatedly I made
requests for a urinal to be kept in my cell. For some years I had
been suffering from more-than-frequent urges to pass urine. In
fact, I need to do so on the average about every half an hour.
The Medical Officer who attended us made a special recommendation to the Camp Commandant to supply me with a urinal,
such as those used in hospitals. Week after week passed, but there
was no response to my request. When I asked the Medical Officer,
he said the authorities had made no provision on their estimates
to purchase piss-pots. When I asked the Commandant, and also
my Case Officer, they both said a piss-pot could not be supplied,
as in the past no detainee had required such a thing. Often I
was in pain, trying to control my urine, my bladder almost at
bursting point as I waited, waited and waited for my turn in the
queue to go to the bathroom each morning and evening. Six of
us shared one bathroom-lavatory. Sometimes the guard had to
seek permission from the Duty N.C.O. to release me to go and
ease myself. I suffered great agony very often, as a result of this
senseless camp arrangement.

As Rahim Ishak, my brother, an M.P. from Singapore, was
coming to see me I told my Case Officer that one complaint I
would certainly be making to him would be about the suffering

I was undergoing as a result of being confined in a cell where normal toilet facilities were denied to me. I put it very strongly, saying that although I was not by nature a complaining man, this infliction on my health I simply could not and would not tolerate. The officer threatened to take action if any complaints I made to my brother were unfounded, or designed to bring discredit on the Special Branch. 'I will answer,' I replied. 'I am prepared for any consequences, as I am the last person to lie about any situation.' Incidentally, this officer had been good enough to allow me to use Japanese-type rubber slippers when, a few days after my confinement, I complained that I did not feel clean, having to walk barefoot from the bathroom to my cell after my ablutions, before my regular prayers there. I learned later on that he paid for the cost of the slippers out of his own pocket. I also discovered that many detainees had made similar requests, but none had received the slippers they asked for. They were only allowed to use slippers when being removed to another camp or place of confinement, after being detained for three months.

Altogether I had spent a month in Cells Nos. 1 and 2. Then, three days before I was to meet my brother Rahim, the authorities moved me to No. 3. It was called The Special. There I was to be confined for the next two months. This place was about thirty-five feet long, half of it being a garden surrounded by a high wall. My living quarters included a wooden platform, used as a bed, a brand-new mattress with kapok filling and new, unused mosquito-nets. (These were given only to me, not to others.) My new house also had two wooden easy-chairs, a table, and two pie-tables; all these pieces of furniture were old and dirty. Anyway they were very welcome to me, but first I had to spend two hours scrubbing the tables and chairs as well as the floor. After all, these belongings were going to keep me company for some time to come; I had no idea at all then how long I would be confined in these new surroundings. The greatest boon of all was a lavatory-cum-shower all my own. No more would I have to suffer through suppressing the flow of urine from my infected bladder! In this haven of solitary confinement, I was given back all my personal belongings, except my razor and spare blades, my mirror, trimming scissors, etc.; in fact any object that could possibly be used as a weapon of self-destruction was withheld. The authorities were afraid I would commit suicide! Another object they did not return was a compass—a tiny instrument, not meant to find my way in either jungle or desert, but rather less spectacularly to orient myself to the direction of Mecca for my prayers. Anyway I could find out this direction easily in my new place by looking up to the sky at the position of the sun.

After some time I asked the Camp Commandant for permission to bring my own pillows, bed-sheets and pillow-cases for comfortable slumber. The camp did not provide such articles, and they gave me permission to have them. Later I found out that my fellow-detainees had to be satisfied with what the camp provided. These restrictions applied until we were all ultimately removed to yet another place of confinement.

One great benefit I enjoyed in The Special was that I had my Koran and other books once again. I began anew with my studies of the Koran, starting from the place where I was interrupted in my reading on the fateful afternoon of 28 January 1965, at my home in Batu Maung.

The day after I arrived in The Special I received an Order from one of the junior Special Branch officers, an Inspector of Police. The Order read:

INTERNAL SECURITY ACT 1960

ORDER OF DETENTION

Section 8 (I) (a)

To:

   PENGUASA,

     TEMPAT TAHANAN KHAS,

      BATU GAJAH.

and to:

The Inspector General of Police, Royal Malaysia Police, all other Police Officers, and all others it may concern.

Whereas the Yang di-Pertuan Agong is satisfied with respect to the undermentioned person that, with a view to preventing that person from acting in any manner Prejudicial to the security of

MALAYSIA/the maintenance of public order therein/the maintenance of essential services therein, it is necessary to make the following order:

Now, therefore, in exercise of the powers conferred upon me by section 8(1) (a) of the Internal Security Act, 1960, I do hereby by this order direct that the undermentioned person forthwith be detained for a period of

TWO YEARS   BATU GAJAH SPECIAL DETENTION CAMP
....in...

or in such other place as I may from time to time direct.

Name of Detainee   *N.R.I.C. No:*
SEL/7290 AZIZ BIN ISHAK   3989202

(Sdg.) DATO' DR. ISMAIL BIN DATO' HAJI
RAHMAN
MENTERI HAL-EHWAL DALAM NEGERI
MALAYSIA

Dated this 22nd day of February, 1965.

MHA. Y. 29/93/

The Special Branch Inspector also gave me the following:

STATEMENT REQUIRED UNDER SECTION
II (2) (b) OF INTERNAL SECURITY ACT
1960

DETAINEE'S NAME: ABDUL AZIZ BIN ISHAK

GROUNDS ON WHICH ORDER OF DETENTION IS MADE

Since 1963, you have consistently acted in a manner which you know to be prejudicial to the security of this country. You have knowingly and willingly plotted with persons whose loyalties are known to be with INDONESIA and collaborated with known Indonesian Intelligence Officers to overthrow the constitutionally elected Malaysian Government by an armed revolution.

ALLEGATIONS OF FACT

Prior to the severance of diplomatic relations between Malaysia and Indonesia, you associated closely with officials of the Indonesian Embassy in KUALA LUMPUR with whom you discussed ways and means, including the use of armed force, to overthrow the Government of this country. You have directed leading members of your NATIONAL CONVENTION PARTY (NCP) to launch Anti-Malaysia campaigns among Malays in the rural areas and to exchange views and information with Indonesian traders who frequented PORT SWETTENHAM.

2. Since OCT 64, you became involved in the activities of the "FRONT NASIONAL," an Indonesian-inspired secret organisation whose aim is to overthrow the Malaysian Government by an armed revolution.

3. You, as one of the leaders of the "FRONT NASIONAL" have made preparations, in accordance with direction which you received from Indonesian Intelligence Officers, to proceed to KARACHI, PAKISTAN with the object of discussing the formation of a Government-in-exile.

By Direction,
Sgd.
b.p. SETIA USAHA,
KEMENTERIAN HAL EHWAL DALAM NEGERI,
MALAYSIA.

I told this officer that I could not accept these allegations against me. I denied categorically all the charges levelled at me, and declared I would seek the advice of a lawyer. I also said, 'I stand by my statement made to the interrogators, as given by me, and not as written by them. I was not shown the statement after it was taken down, nor was I asked to put my signature to it.' Later I was to find out that my version of my alleged involvement was not accepted by the Special Branch and the Government. About ten days after receiving the Order and the Charge, my lawyer, an old friend, Encik K.L. Devaser, addressed familiarly by me as Lal, came to see me, accompanied by my son, Zakaria. During our interview this time there were no Special Branch officers present, but there was probably no need—I suspect the room was bugged. Surely the Special Branch could not be so trustingly naive! Sometimes they seemed to want to give us that impression. Within the one hour allotted me, I told Lal exactly but briefly the extent of my involvement in the plan of the Government to arrest the Opposition. So as not to reveal in detail my involvement or otherwise, it was best for the time being to say that my only involvement was a technical one—in that I had not reported to the authorities that I had been approached by a few members of the Opposition to leave the country. It was sufficient for the Government that I had given the Special Branch a pretended excuse to arrest me. Already it had been disclosed in public statements made by two detainees that I did not want to accept their invitation to leave Malaysia. But the authorities seemed bent on making all the allegations look as black as possible—that I was a wicked and deceitful person, a tool of the Indonesians and, therefore, disloyal and treacherous to the Government in power. God only knows the truth! Human beings will also know it only in God's own time!

It is well-known that people in positions of power usually call anyone *mad* or *wrong* whose standards differ from their own. This was true in my own case, as opposed to that of my former colleagues in the Government. Only in the process they transformed me from being mad to being *wrong* in having given them this opportunity. My advice to anyone in circumstances such as mine would be not to allow himself to fall into the trap in which I had been caught. I had realized all along, even before my arrest, that the good suffer on account of their very goodness, the evil ones on account of their evil. But the balance will be set right in the end, and not necessarily only after death.

IX. FRUSTRATION

In The Special, my third place of confinement, I was more lonely than in either of the other two detention places, because I was left very much to myself. I know now only too well what solitary confinement means. Visits from the guards occurred only three times a day, when they had to bring my meals. If your time is not fully occupied you are inclined to feel the growing weight of utter solitude. Sometimes I would count the days to arrive at seven, the magic figure, waiting for the weekly visits from my children living in Kuala Lumpur. My wife came to see me once every three weeks. These visits did not always bring joy. After these meetings, any bad news would make me moody and unhappy. Generally speaking, however, I was much more often very cheerful at heart after seeing members of my family.

When my detention began, my family's financial position was at its lowest ebb, but suddenly the tide changed, as help came from many quarters. My children were employed with better salaries and prospects, and friends and relatives helped to contribute to my family's expenses. In my own mind, my foremost hopes were not financial gain for either myself or my family, but rather their spiritual elevation. I wanted very much to rehabilitate them all; they would be the first to receive my attention. I managed to achieve this reform in small doses during their weekly visits. Usually, however, just to discuss religious matters was too boring for their liking. Unless I took care to vary my conversation to include lighter topics and other matters, they might find it a trial to see me once a week. So whenever we met, I always kept this in mind. Ours is a happy family. We always enjoy good jokes about ourselves and other people, as long as they are not vicious. Very often the Special Branch policemen or officers attending any of our interviews found these quite amusing. Our meetings were punctuated with continuous roars of laughter. Sometimes an officer would try to join in our conversation, but this did not happen often; we thought it tactless.

There is an attitude of mind common to some Special Branch officers I encountered during my detention, an attitude I thought objectionable. They seemed to have the impression that they even owned my thoughts! They wanted to control them. Had they any right to do so? Nothing in me seemed completely my own. Such types act and think as if they are not born plain mortals like me; they are not like other people—after all they are carefully selected by Special Branch to fulfil a mission. I feel rather sorry for them. In weaker moments, meeting such people is inclined to shake one's trust in God, but after all, looked at correctly, it is merely a trial of one's own faith. God does not grant to every one of his servants a nature and character that can always rise above shafts of doubt or grief, or suffering due either to slander or persecution.

After my transfer to The Special, I received food regularly from home—sometimes it was *briani* rice from Bilal's or Kassim's Restaurants, but always and without fail there came from home, curry with beef, mutton, chicken, liver, spleen, or heart, etc. cooked just the way I liked best. Sometimes these delights were varied with *laksa*, *mee* or *kwey tiow*. My family always brought home-cooked food with them whenever I went to meet them at the High Street Police Station.

On one occasion, my old father, Encik Ishak bin Ahmad, became quite ill and wished to see me, so my brother Rahim made a special request for me to be taken to the family house at Gombak, 6 miles from the city. After this, on his subsequent visits to High Street the usual first-floor room was not used, as my father could not climb the stairs. Special arrangements were also made for him to give me useful discussions on religion in the presence of four Special Branch officers, two with rank and two without. On such occasions I would be treated to various meals, including *murtabak*, in which the officers would join politely.

Often I brought back to the camp, mutton curry, cakes, chocolates, cheese and biscuits; even paperbacks about Perry Mason or James Bond, all presents from my sister, Alma Azizah, and my brother-in-law, Dr. Johan Thambu.

My father felt greatly cheered when I responded to his reminder that everything that had happened was by the will of God. So there was no necessity to worry about it, except to submit to His Will. He also said, 'The Government of God is the supreme Government, and every action is an act made with God's will and knowledge!'

It gave me great joy to learn from my sister and brother-in-law, who were living with my father, that they had told him they believed in my sincerity, no matter what I had been accused of doing. They did not think I could be capable of anything blatantly dishonest. This is true, as very early in life my father taught me, 'Honour in the sight of God is not due to race, or to profession of faith, but to sincere and righteous conduct.' He also said, 'It is not enough just to know this adage but also to practise it, and to teach it to others as well.'

There was one change that I experienced during my detention, a change of heart and mind that affects me even now. I was to discover that I had no feelings of bitterness whatsoever, only surprise and wonder at the extent of human good. Some want to go to Heaven. Some expect other forms of reward, either in wealth or other attributes coming from God or man. But the real reward for good, or for doing good, is good itself. Does not one feel good when one does good for no other reason than for the sake of good? If our minds dwell on this truth and can accept it, then evil will not dare come near us.

It is unnecessary to report, either in praise or otherwise, on the food supplied at the Federal Holding Centre. From the beginning there were several grades of detainees. There were those who could authoritatively demand apples, or to be given newspapers to read, as a right; there were others who would be given only bread and jam or margarine. It is futile to say more, especially when everyone knows that the Government from time to time publicizes the cost of maintaining a detainee in the Federal Holding Centre, or in a detention camp, or anywhere else. But it was quite a different story when we came to be housed in the annexe of Pudu Gaol in Kuala Lumpur after being incarcerated in the Federal Holding Centre for over three months. We were fated to stay at this new place for nearly nine months before we were finally released. A detainee only left his cell to be led out for interrogation, or to see a doctor, and then back again he would go into his cell—always in haste, and always under close guard. During the hurried periods of taking exercise, about five minutes each morning, this again depending on the availability of time or space, a small enclosure would be reserved for this purpose. At The Special one could only see the sky above a wall about twenty-five to thirty feet high.

I got tired of trying to guess where I was, and gave it up as time-wasting and unnecessary, unless of course I was planning to escape. But no such idea ever entered my mind, despite my having read many wartime escape stories in books or having seen them in cinemas. Perhaps if I was younger at the time I might have given serious thought to the idea of escaping, but my mind was occupied with thoughts that were much more lasting and more valuable to me. I was thinking not of physical escape but of a spiritual one.

X. MY CO-DETAINEES

CONFINED as I was with the minimum of comfort or movement, my lonely days and nights seemed unending. In normal life during middle-age the days seem to pass by very quickly, so much so that one looks back with deep affection to childhood and early youth, when each day was very long and very full and happy. Not so in a cell. Each day and night drags by wearily with the weight of passing minutes, each hour seeming longer than the last. No wonder, therefore, that I sought spiritual escape in reading the Koran and thinking of my Faith, my family, my own immediate concerns and wondering about my future. To keep one's control, one's calm, yes, even one's sanity, the only refuge and relief is to keep the mind busy. I had another constant worry in these days of confinement. What had happened to my friends? Where were those arrested the day before me? What else was going on? Alone, under constant guard, I had no way of knowing. I could talk only to my guards or to my Case Officers—no one else. Naturally I could expect to learn little from these men. It is part of their training not to talk, except about essential needs. Of course, I did get to know some things about the outside world from my family, or from Lal Devaser, but it was all relating to myself.

One important thing—important to me because it did not add to whatever peace of mind I retained despite myself—I did learn, and from the least expected quarter. *From my Case Officers!* During my interrogation one day they told me a certain fact. They did so because it was another weapon in their armoury of persuasion. They said, 'Datuk Raja Abu Hanifah and Ishak Haji Mohamed have confessed. So why should you not do so?' I was neither deterred nor deluded by this line of approach. Had they not begun to realize even yet that the answers I had given to their questions were honest? Did they really expect me to break down and tell some other story that would fit in with the confessions? As far as I was concerned, how did I know whether this statement about the confessions was fiction or fact? If it was fiction, they must think me a fool indeed. If it was fact, then what did it matter? My story was mine; their stories were theirs. At this point we reached a stalemate. If they were disappointed they did not betray their feelings. I did not care one jot. I had answered all they had asked with the truth as I saw and knew it. In fact they knew that I was not guilty. If they had to fit my statements into a neat jigsaw with alleged confessions, that was their problem, not mine.

Back in my cell, of course, this revelation, if it was true, naturally set me wondering. Any man would feel the same in my circumstances. But the niggling thought was there. If they had confessed, had they involved me? I did not believe it possible. So I decided, just as I had with my approach to my family, just as I had with my spiritual renewal, that it was necessary always to have faith. And common sense had something else to add to this resolution. I could not be betrayed, because there was nothing to betray! The time would come when I would know what had actually happened—of that I felt certain. Before I could know the fate of my friends and of others I would just have to be patient and wait—wait—wait. It would finally come out.

And come out it did, with a completely new turn of events. One evening—it was 26 April 1965—a Police Sergeant, the most senior NCO in The Special, came to see me. He said I was to make myself ready to move, that I was leaving The Special at once. His manner was rather non-committal. What did this mean? My release? Another destination? Further confinement? If so, where? Release seemed too much to hope for; more likely another place, the Batu Gajah Detention Camp perhaps? So my thinking ran, because the Detention Order I had received had stated I might be detained at Batu Gajah or any other detention camp for a period of two years. It was night, so probably I was going by train. This news left me feeling very uncertain. I tried to get more information out of the Police Sergeant, and also from the policeman who brought me my evening meal. No luck. They both seemed to be unaware of anything. The only crumb I gleaned was this; the Police Sergeant hinted that it would be a better place than the present one. With that I had to remain content.

An hour or so passed. It was eight o'clock, just before *Isha*, the last regular prayer of the evening. I was ready with what small possessions I had. They led me to another Black Maria. Off we started, my mind imagining all sorts of things, my heart throbbing fast. The journey lasted about half an hour. When we finally stopped and I got out, there I was at Kuala Lumpur's Pudu Gaol. Back where I started, I thought. What would happen next? They ushered me into an annexe. To my surprise and delight, there were Datuk Raja Abu Hanifah and Ishak Haji Mohamed coming to welcome me. They seemed a little uncertain of how to greet me, not knowing what my reactions might be. I quickly put them at their ease by being rather cordial to both, recalling inwardly at the same time they were supposed to have confessed. Soon I was to know what had happened.

They, too, had been confined in The Special where I had been without any of us knowing of the others' presence there. They had earned entry into The Special because both had already confessed. I had been placed in the same confinement area because of my threats to inform my younger brother, Rahim Ishak, of the bad treatment I had received in both my first and second cells in two other places. Now we were together again—and I mean together. We were not confined in the gaol itself, but the three of us were to share two bungalows, originally built for senior prison officers and later converted into an Internal Training Wing for officers across the street, looking out over Jalan Shaw, a busy traffic artery running north-south in Kuala Lumpur.

One blessing at least! No more solitary. At last I could feel truly human again. Companionship, freedom to talk, living in a house, more room to move and breathe, even able to see the cars whizzing by and people coming and going in the street! It seemed too good to be true—but it was still confinement.

But what had happened to my friends? Datuk Raja Hanifah, who had been the Supervisor of the election campaign in 1964 for the P.M.I.P. (Pan-Malayan Islamic Party), was formerly an M.P. for Pasir Mas, Kelantan. He was one of the four arrested on 27 January 1965. Briefly, this was his story of the past months since his arrest. As I learned it from him, he was involved only personally, not his party, the P.M.I.P. He had been arrested on his return from Tokyo where he had met an Indonesian politician. He confessed that he had received a certain amount of money, but not the amount alleged by the Government, which was considerably more than he had actually obtained. However he did not tell me very much more of what actually took place, apart from what had already been given to the Press before I myself was arrested. I did not insist on Datuk Raja Abu Hanifah giving me more details of what happened to him. But he did confess that he had received and accepted money from Indonesia.

Ishak Haji Mohamed, popularly known as Pak Sako, had a different story to tell. He was the Chairman of the Socialist Front at one time, and was replaced by Hasnul Abdul Hadi. He was arrested on the same day that I was, but I had no knowledge of this until much later. He told me he confessed he had also received money during the 1964 elections, but again the amount was very much less than the Special Branch accused him of having accepted. During the first month of their detention both Datuk Raja and Ishak had broadcast over Radio Malaysia detailing their involvement in the allegations against them. They did this after being assured that they would soon be released following their public confession. This promise of release made to them led to some quiet thinking on my own situation. We had all been arrested within a few days. We had all undergone interrogation, brief in their cases, but long in mine. They had confessed, I had not, for I was not involved. They had even gone on the air, I had not. If they were to be released, what would happen to me? Would I go too, at the same time? They had some hope, I had been given none. They had a promise, I did not. They believed they would be set free soon because they had confessed. But it was not to be.

In the end we were, each and all of us, to learn bitterly the value of a promise made, or believed to have been made, by those in power. We did not know it then, but the future was to be more unendurable in many ways than what we had already suffered, as my story reveals. Since the time of the arrest we had been detained for four months. By the time of our ultimate release we would have served more than a year!

PART II

*In statesmanship, get the formalities right,
never mind about the moralities.*

MARK TWAIN, *Pudd'n-head Wilson's Calendar*

PART II

*In statesmanship, get the formalities right,
never mind about the moralities.*

Mark Twain, *Pudd'n-head Wilson's Calendar*

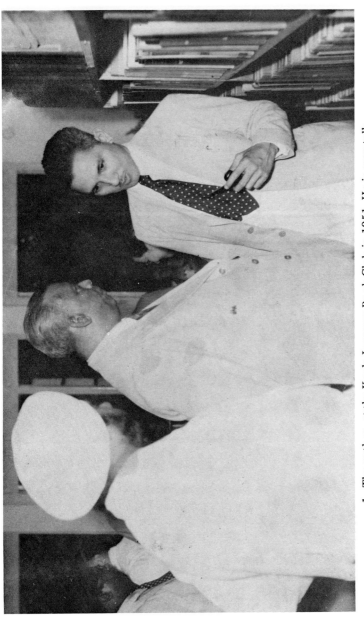

1 The author, at the Kuala Lumpur Book Club in 1951. He is seen talking to Dato Sir Clough Thuraisingam, later to become Member for Education in 1954 soon before the Elections in 1955.

2 The author, who was Head of the Delegation for the United Kingdom at the F.A.O. Regional Conference at Bandung in 1956. A British Agricultural Officer is seen in the background. At this conference the author was elected Deputy Chairman of the F.A.O. Regional Conference for Asia and the Far East.

3 The author is seen taking part in the first *gotong royong* project, in Perlis, in 1958. This was a precursor to subsequent rural development projects in the country.

4 A picture taken in July 1957, on the author's arrival at the New Delhi Airport, on a visit to India to study Community Development. From left to right: the author, Malcolm MacDonald, unidentified Indian official, Lady Mountbatten, and Pandit Nehru, Prime Minister of India.

5 The swearing in ceremony of the author, Malaya's Independence Day, 31 August 1957. Tunku Abdul Rahman, the then Prime Minister, is seen in the background.

6 The first Cabinet of Tunku Abdul Rahman Putra, taken with the first
   Yang Dipertuan Agung, 31 August 1957.

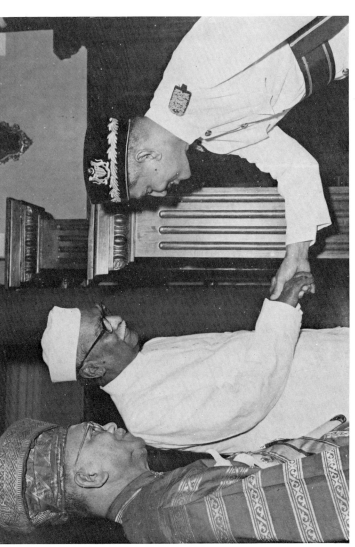

7 The visit of the President of India in 1957, when the author acted as Minister in Attendance. The first Yang Dipertuan Agung, Tuanku Abdul Rahman of Negri Sembilan, is on the right of the President—Rajendra Prasad.

8 In Johor Bahru in 1962, on the occasion of the opening of the Federal Poultry Centre by H.H. the Sultan of Johor. In the foreground is the Indian Minister of Agriculture, Dr. Ram Singh Subagh.

I. THE HEARING

SOMETIMES life lands us in the oddest situations, specially in relation to people one has just met for the first time. Most people, I think, would agree that any friendly feelings between a detainee and a Special Branch officer would be most unlikely, especially in custody. That is not my experience. During my new period of detention in Jalan Shaw I met one officer, among others, who became more than an acquaintance, in fact, almost a friend. Our association began badly, but ended well. He kept entering and leaving my caged life.

Uppermost in the minds of all three of us—Datuk Raja, Ishak and I—was the question of release. It always hung in the air. When would it take place? Soon? In two years? Or never? To understand our feelings it is necessary to know about practice and procedure in matters of detention. As the weeks and months passed by, I came to learn more about the problem of release or otherwise by talking with several officers in the Special Branch, Selangor.

The first aspect of the problem is, of course, 'Who is the authority responsible? Who decides?' The answer was not simple, as I was to learn from one Special Branch officer who set out for me in detail what happened from the time a detainee first came under close surveillance until his arrest. Obviously, after what I had come through, much of what he said was no news to me, but some of it was. New information is always useful, sooner or later, as any journalist knows. Being one myself, I was all ears. What was the procedure after arrest? This was what I wanted to learn, and the facts were very interesting indeed; so much so it was ironic to remember that, like most people, I had often spoken of living my own life. This was what happened to a detainee.

After arrest until his Order of Detention is made out, a detainee is completely under the authority of the Special Branch, and strictly so, with 'no political interference by anyone'. The Special Branch then reports to the Ministry of Internal Security that a detainee is implicated, and therefore recommends detention, for say, two years. In fact, always for two years. After this Order is served on the detainee, his fate is entirely at the will and pleasure of the Minister of Internal Security and of the Prime Minister. But this rigid procedure can be tampered with even before the Special Branch has enough evidence to recommend that a person should be picked up. In fact, it can occur from above. Those at the top can ask the Special Branch to devise a plan to detain so-and-so. This can happen even in a Government that claims to practise democracy.

Under the law in times of emergency, at least in Malaya, there is also an Advisory Board, to which a detainee may appeal at specific periods. Strictly speaking, a detainee, after receiving an Order for a prescribed period of detention, can be released by the Minister of Internal Security, or the Cabinet, or the Prime Minister himself. The Advisory Board is only a façade. Its members are citizens who have undivided loyalty to the Prime Minister. The Chairman, however well-meaning he may be, is in fact powerless if the Minister has his own plans for a detainee.

I was in the unique position of knowing all these things, having been in the Alliance Cabinet for over seven years, not to mention my own personal experience of Special Branch machinery during the first Emergency, 1948–60, as well as what I was now garnering from Special Branch officers during my detention. So whenever an officer tried to pass the buck to the Board, to the Cabinet, or even to God, as an excuse for inaction or a reason for action, I was not particularly impressed.

In short, too many reasons were volunteered at various times to explain why we were detained for so many months after we had been told that we would be released in a matter of a few weeks, or even days. Procrastination is the thief of time, so the proverb says. The Special Branch, we soon found out, was a master of that: always we were waved away; always there would be another glib explanation. At first we felt unhappy, then finally disgusted, over the non-fulfilment of the promise which the Special Branch had made to release us. We had moved into the Jalan Shaw bungalow on 26 April 1965. We had been told that the Advisory Board would be hearing our cases on 5 May 1965. We fully believed that we would be released soon after the Board heard our cases. So we only had ten days more to wait—and then, freedom! Patiently we waited for the day, but confirmation had to come first. We knew that from past experience. A promise, or information, did not always mean performance. The Special Branch acts in its own mysterious ways. It could happen—it might not. When confirmation finally did arrive, of course it came quite suddenly—to our surprise and relief the hearing *would* be on 5 May. I had barely fifteen minutes to talk with my friend and lawyer, Lal Devaser, who had very kindly agreed to represent me at the hearing. At first it had been arranged that I would be given a whole day to meet and consult with him, before appearing at the Board's hearing. Somehow this arrangement fell through. Perhaps it was the fault of the Special Branch again!

A former Appeal Court Judge, Mr. Justice D.W.B. Good, was the Chairman of the Board. There were two other members. One was an old football crony of Tunku Abdul Rahman, who was President of both the Football Association of Malaysia and of the Asian Football Confederation. He was brusque, and even directly rude. The other member was an Eurasian businessman from Ipoh; he was not so vocal.

Mr. Good knew me personally. In fact he had taught me English Literature at Raffles Institution in Singapore in the early thirties. He was a man who had won high esteem in the legal world and his bearing matched his reputation.

When the Board's session began, my two co-detainees went first—each separately, each hearing taking half an hour. When I was called, the time was 10.30 a.m. My hearing lasted three hours. From the beginning I denied completely all the allegations contained in the Order of Detention. Mr. Devaser then asked if there were any further allegations other than those contained in the Order. Mr. Good replied that there were three more which showed my implication in the indictment.

First—two Indonesians were reported to have visited my house at Morib during the month of April 1963. I admitted this was so, and named the two Indonesians. They were Dr. Takdir Alisjahbana, Professor of Malay Studies, University of Malaya, and Encik Idros, an editor of the U.S.I.S. Journal. 'Both of them are well-known for their anti-Soekarno activities,' I said. Mr. Good did not comment on my remarks. Obviously he knew this to be true, but with tongue-in-cheek read the report merely to indicate that the allegations against me were numerous, without actually confirming their veracity.

The second charge was that I had consorted with a Chinese Assistant Editor of the *Malaysian Times*, and that we had arranged together to land arms from Indonesia. Mr. Good mentioned this man's name, but I cannot remember it even now. He was supposed to have visited my home in Morib in 1963. This charge was also a complete fabrication, for I did not know this Chinese newspaperman at all; his name meant nothing to me! The Special Branch officer who received and made this report must have been highly irresponsible, to say the least. If true, it was a very serious allegation indeed. I said as much to the members of the Board, and Mr. Good remarked that the report should have been confirmed. But why was I hearing about it now for the first time at this interview with the Board? 'Why was this matter not raised during my interrogation?' I asked Mr. Good. He made no comment.

Lastly I was alleged to have made a speech in Kampung Raja Uda, Selangor, in November 1963, calling for the downfall of the Alliance Government through armed insurrection. Again, another highly irresponsible statement! According to Mr. Good himself, perhaps it had been a report made to the Special Branch by someone not actually working for them. Mr. Devaser then drew the conclusion that my alleged involvement was only a technical one. I should have reported at the time that overtures had been made to me to go overseas. He also pointed out that I had refused the invitation to leave the country. This fact had been borne out at my interrogation.

However, the version given to the public as propaganda was totally different. After my release I was informed (and confirmed what I heard by reading back numbers of the *Straits Times*) that the Prime Minister and other Alliance leaders during the time of my detention, in several speeches around the country, had made capital of my alleged implication, condemning me when they knew quite well that I was not involved. The Special Branch, therefore, had served both them and me with a false report of involvement. Certainly someone was responsible for this diabolical act! Anyway, when rudely pressed by the Indian member, I said, 'For my sins of omission I repent!' He remarked, 'You don't look like a person who is repentant.' I replied, 'I am—one repents for one's faults, or mistakes, or sins, if one is a good Muslim. I am doing just that—but only to God!'

During the interview with the Board, Mr. Good tried to convince me about a charge I had made at my interrogation that one of the detainees was a double agent, working for the Special Branch, with the result that my arrest and detention were wrong. He said he had personally examined the case of this man and had found that he was not a Special Branch informer. I did not comment, since I had not brought the subject up. Apropos of nothing, it had been introduced by Mr. Good himself. In fact I recall now, as I did then, that this man was a fellow detainee. I identified him by his voice, when shouting with a high note of authority at police guards outside our cells (when I was in Cell No. 1). He was demanding his ration of apples and two boiled eggs. I, on the other hand, was getting only a slice of bread and jam. Later in The Special I would get one egg, a banana or a slice of pineapple, but never once a single apple! The reference to this man by Mr. Good ended the sitting of the Advisory Board. According to the wording of the invitation, the title 'Notice of Hearing of Representation' sounded grandly democratic! The actual time taken for my case lasted not less than three hours. My colleagues were heard for half an hour each. Because of their confessions, I suppose.

Later, I pressed one Special Branch officer to tell me what authority the Advisory Board had after hearing our cases to recommend our release. He replied laconically, 'None.' I had known this to be so all along when I was an Alliance Cabinet Minister. Hence it is easy to assess in what esteem I held the worth of the Advisory Board!

II. HOPE DELAYED

THE Board session over, we lived from day to day waiting to hear the results. When would we be released, if at all? We had to know, our suppressed feelings might come to boiling-point! A week went by, a fretful seven days, but no news yet! Any expectations we had of a swift decision were now dissipated. With all our political experience, perhaps we should have known better. The mills of law or Government grind slowly. It is easy to be patient when you are a free man—not so easy when you are caged. The weeks went by—one, two, three, a month—unrelenting days, and still no further news. Slowly our spirits dropped. There was hardly any experience more shattering than hope delayed, even more so if hope was frustrated.

Datuk Raja, forty-two years old, is normally a quiet-spoken, calm man. I could see increasing signs of irritability. Encik Ishak, at fifty-eight, reacted quite differently. He became rather restless, walked about moodily, and often talked in his sleep. Even I, then fifty, and the coolest of the three, was trying my best to control my disappointment, but without much success. We had every reason to feel deeply depressed. It was now early June, a month since the hearing. 5 June dragged on to 12 June, then 19 June—another two weeks, six now since we had appeared before the Board. Would it never end? Were they ever going to tell us?

We did not realize it then, but the result of the hearing had already been decided, and the information was now on its way to us. We had forgotten that the machinery of Government must go through official channels. Even if we did think of this, we brushed it aside, for we had only one thought—freedom!

I will never forget—nor will either Datuk Raja or Ishak—the day of 22 June. At about 3.00 p.m. our Duty Sergeant came in.

He had three letters and handed one to each of us. We opened them. Reading mine, I was shocked, incredulous, astounded. The letter to me from the Ministry of Home Affairs, dated 12 June, read:

'I am directed to inform you that the representation made by you under Section 11 (1) of the Internal Security Act 1960 was heard by the Advisory Board on 5.5.1965. After considering the Report and Recommendation of the Advisory Board, the D.Y.M.M. Seri Paduka Baginda Yang di-Pertuan Agong has decided that the Order of Detention/Restricted Order which was issued against you on 22.2.1965 should continue to remain in force.'

I looked up, feeling stunned. I saw the others—Ishak sitting stiffly in a chair as if he were at attention, Datuk Raja half-sitting, half-lying on his bed. There was no need to speak—shock gleamed in their startled eyes. Chattering in amazement, we compared letters; each had received the same, only the names differed. It was over, all hope of release gone! A silence fell on us—deadly like despair. We simply could not believe what we had read. There was nothing to do or say. I sat gloomily in my chair, Ishak had his hands over his bent head, Datuk Raja was now lying back, staring at the ceiling. I would not say he boiled over—he burst open! Suddenly he started shouting—cursing, swearing, crying, calling the Government all the names under the sun. He raged without stopping, yelling at the top of his voice, and all the time lying or rolling about on his bed. Never had I seen such passion, such towering rage, in any man. On and on he went for ten minutes, Ishak and I staring at him. And then he stopped, and turned his face to the wall. Ishak got up and walked quickly out of the room. He did not return for nearly half an hour. I was still sitting in the same position in my chair when he came back. My mind was in a whirl, I couldn't think, I didn't know what to do. Then I realized it was four in the afternoon, time for prayer. So I prayed.

I must have looked at the letter again—I don't remember exactly—for I then saw the date. 12 June, and it was now 22 June. Ten days for the letter to reach me! It had gone through the official channels. Of course, things must be done properly, I thought bitterly. It had taken five weeks from the date of the hearing of the Board to the writing of the letter. As if that delay was not enough, it went first to the Commandant at the Batu Gajah Detention Camp, 100 miles away, and then had been sent on in the usual manner, just another routine job. That was why it had taken ten days. During the whole of that time since 5 May the Special Branch had not dropped the slightest hint, although they must have known! 'Dear God,' I thought, 'and people talk of the dignity of man!'

So we returned to the inevitable round of nights and days in detention. Those were the hardest weeks of all, having to adjust ourselves to this dire turn of the wheel of Fate. How my friends felt inwardly I would never know, but it was evident to me that Datuk Raja was no longer the calm man he used to be. If anything he was moodier than Ishak. If our bungalow had been happy by comparison just after the 5 May hearing, it was certainly a sad house now. I am sure that even the guards on duty outside, or the ever-present NCOs inside, must have felt our clouds of depression.

It was too much to expect that this state of mind could continue unbroken. It didn't. Early in July, only two weeks after his first outburst of rage, Datuk Raja burst out again. He had gone to see his wife and family at the High Street Police Station. There, despite the presence of Special Branch officers during this visit, he broke down in fits of temper. He did it on purpose. Obviously he had been building up a head of steam for the past fortnight. He exploded! In an hysterical outburst he condemned the Special Branch, the Prime Minister, and the whole machinery of Government. Of course, every word was reported to the highest authorities in Special Branch, or perhaps even higher. But Datuk Raja did not care, he had gotten his rage out of his system. But not completely; after the letters, Datuk Raja never really tried to make anything of the kind of life we had to live, whether we liked it or not. As the days dragged by, seemingly without end, no light of hope in the distance, his detention slowly defeated him. It was little wonder to me, therefore, considering all the circumstances, that two months later, in September, with still no news of release, Datuk Raja became so ill that he had to be admitted to the General Hospital in Kuala Lumpur. And he was the youngest of us! A contributing cause of his illness was undoubtedly the food we had. As if the frustration of knowing nothing, of never hearing anything, was not enough to try our self-control, the food provided gradually became worse and worse. It seemed to be nobody's business to make a check. Several times I complained, rather tactfully, to our custodian A.S.P. about the bad food, with a sincere hope that the contractor would be cautioned, and so improve his supplies.

One morning—it was three weeks after the letters—when we saw the food brought to us, we refused to eat it, telling the man to take it back. He ignored our request; so we did not touch it. Instead we sent a policeman, who was just going off duty, to buy some *nasi padang*, a Sumatran-type food, from a restaurant nearby. I told this man to report our refusal to eat to his superior officer at High Street, but he came back saying the officer there was on leave. Then we told him to report our action to the next most senior officer.

Our pent-up feelings, together with the bad food, were bound to lead to another explosion, sooner or later. Our refusal to eat that day lit the fuse! On that very afternoon a senior Special Branch officer from Bluff Road Headquarters came to our bungalow. He wanted to find out what our actual motives were in rejecting the food. Obviously the police feared we were behaving like this for political reasons. After some explanations, he accepted our quite sincere protests that the quality of the food was bad and the cooking indifferent. This officer was known as a tough character. Perhaps that was why he was sent to investigate. Incidentally, this very officer was one of those who had told us that we would be released soon after an assessment of our behaviour had been made. During our conversation, I remarked, quite deliberately, 'If we were of another race, not Malay, perhaps we would have been released earlier.' I wanted to show him that we had discussed among ourselves the probable reasons why the authorities did not fulfil their promise to release us. I knew myself of cases of several detainees of other races who, after making public their intention to abjure politics, had been released immediately. But this had not happened to either Datuk Raja or Ishak, even though they had confessed.

'The Government's treatment of us,' I said, 'is probably because we are considered unimportant in their reckoning or classification. Malays are generally treated in such a manner all the time.'

Then the officer, the tough talker, really lost his temper. He

shouted threats that I could be charged for trying to say that
the Government was making our cases a communal issue. Of
course, I promptly shouted back, declaring, 'I am merely indicat-
ing to you how our minds come to arrive at this conclusion.'
Then he dared me to put it down in writing. To his utter surprise,
I agreed most readily to do so. Later on he forgot all about his
dare. He realised that I was in earnest and that I was not going
to be browbeaten by any threats of his.

The next day I was sent for. Naturally, I thought that our
complaints were being taken up seriously. At the interview, this
tough character being present, I referred to the heated incident
between us in a joking kind of way, and this led to mutual apolo-
gies, quite like gentlemen in a grand manner.

As a result of our protests, we immediately got a new caterer.
Later I learned that our custodian A.S.P., who arranged this, told
the proprietor of the new restaurant to supply us with the best,
as we were police officers from Sabah taking a course in Kuala
Lumpur! The food was much better, but alas, only for three
weeks! Then it deteriorated again. We had to give reminders continually about keeping the fare up to standard. We never did
discover how much it cost to supply us with food, which in our
case was only lunch and dinner. At breakfast-time we cooked our
own porridge and ate bread and butter. Sometimes we fried eggs
or made tomato omelettes, varied by sardines. When we felt like
a change in diet we used to spend our own money to buy *roti
perata* or *nasi lemak*, or even *tossay*, a South Indian food. Very
often we shared our breakfast with the policeman on duty. I always
prepared the breakfast, whilst Datuk Raja washed the plates after
meals. Ishak's job was to sweep the floor and clean the lavatory,
which he seemed to take pleasure in doing. In fact, during the
last three months before we were finally released our food was
quite good. Occasionally, when one of us received money from
home, we would arrange a *briani* feast. All this high living, of
course, only took place towards the later part of our detention
in Shaw Road. As far as I am concerned, Shaw Road was, in
spite of tribulations, more comfortable than my two previous detention homes. In Cells Nos. 1 and 2 I never saw a newspaper,
I was not allowed to listen to the radio, and whatever news I

did acquire about what was going on in the world outside came to me only in the visits to High Street to meet my wife and family. What was even worse, especially for a journalist, a man who always likes to write, I was not allowed to receive any mail at all. They permitted me to write to my wife once a week, and these personal letters had to be handed over unsealed so that they could be censored.

At Shaw Road we were in better touch with the world. We could see people going by and they could see us from the road. We asked once if we could visit a cinema. There were two movie houses only a few hundred yards away. They rejected our request. But we did get one surprise, just after Datuk Raja broke down for the first time. To our amazement suddenly a T.V. set was installed in our lounge. From then on we were able to watch this box during broadcasting hours in the evening if we felt so inclined. I suspect, however, that it was as much an amenity for our guards as for us, because they too must have been equally bored by the dull daily routine. Human memory being what it is, one becomes inclined to forget the hardships one experiences, even if these are only recent. So whenever I made any statements after my release I did not want to give any wrong impression by over-praising the comfort of our Shaw Road period. What is the yardstick of comfort, anyway?

III. OUR DOCTORS

AFTER the abortion of the original plan to release us—was it ever a plan, I wonder?—our hopes of freedom seemed to disappear altogether; they were like ghosts sent to haunt us. Our daily round became deadly dull routine; we had lost all enthusiasm. Finally, we reached the stage of resigning ourselves to the fact that we would have to live out the two full years prescribed by the Order of Detention. It even seemed possible—who knew?—that the period might be extended, as had happened before in the cases of Ahmad Boestamam and others. 'When, when will our freedom come?' That nagging thought, the one and only question, was ever and always in our minds.

Only one bright ray of hope ever come our way. That was the day in August 1965 when we heard the news of the sudden separation of Singapore from Malaysia. Buoyant again, we thought it would lead to our release much sooner than we expected. No such luck; another hope frustrated!

After we had surrendered all hope of early release, I began to plan a more orderly programme in detention. After all, we had to keep going, protect our health and well-being, exercise our bodies and minds. Reading and recreation could keep us fit. There was no sense in leading a passive life; we must keep active. We were men with families, and so naturally we all wanted to return home in good condition—whenever we did get out. It was obvious to me that for men of our age any strenuous exercise might do more harm than good. If we tried skipping, for instance, our ankles and knees would swell, and it would take months to get them back to normal. Our doctor had forbidden any strenuous exercise, in case any of us might be struck by a heart attack. His opinion seemed to frighten the Special Branch. Readily they agreed that we needed exercise. We asked for a ping-pong table, yet they could not get any money to grant our request. However, I asked if I could use my golf clubs to knock a few plastic balls about inside the compound. They consented, rather reluctantly, I thought, and, as was usual with any of their decisions, set a restriction—I was not to do so in broad daylight.

Up to this time, about the end of June, we had obediently followed a Standing Instruction not to show ourselves in the compound of our bungalow during the day. After our repeated disappointments over not being released, we became independent; our mood was 'Come what may! Couldn't care less!' Openly we ignored the order, and spent as much time as possible in the garden. Oddly enough, and greatly to our surprise, the Special Branch officers who came to visit us did not seem to mind very much when they saw us outside.

This reaction encouraged us further. Now I became bold enough to ask if I could hit real golf-balls in an open space. Diagonally across the road from our compound was a football field, belonging to the Prisons' Department. It was about 140 yards long, just right for golf practice. We got permission, but again reluctantly. I rather suspect one of our A.S.P.s had not received authority from his superior officer, as once when I mentioned I was taking golf exercise early in the morning with a policeman standing nearby, he looked at me blankly, making no comment. So I continued with my mini-golf right up to the time of my release.

During the whole period of our detention we had medical attention from three doctors. The first doctor came for about five months, and then left Government service. We thought him rather a joke. Being young, he treated us with respect, and that is all to his credit as a man, but as a doctor he was not much help to us. He would tell me my heart ticked so well it was like that of a person under thirty. At first, and for some time afterwards, I felt rather braced by this opinion. Then by comparing notes with others I found out that he had been saying the same thing to all the detainees. It was just a stock phrase of his. During the early period of my detention I suffered from various minor illnesses or physical disabilities, such as backache or difficulty in urinating—the latter most of all, being an ailment of many years' standing and having to pass water frequently owing to a disorder

of the bladder. In each case I received the same medicine. I
mentioned this to my two friends in Shaw Road. They replied that
they, too, were getting identical medicines for other complaints
different from mine. So thereafter we named him 'Dr. A.P.C.'

Next we had his successor—a perfect man and doctor—always
polite to all, and very thorough in his examinations. Each time
he made a diagnosis, it was the proper and correct one for the
particular illness. He made sure we had a continuous supply of
vitamins, laxatives, cough-drops or embrocation. He mentioned
that when he was doing his housemanship in the United States
he used to play golf. When he learned I was starting to play again,
he gave me some new golf-balls.

Our third doctor acted as his locum tenens or stand-in. He,
too, was most competent—a very kind, friendly and painstaking
man. So, it is a fair comment that we received the best medical
attention from these two.

For me, however, during my dreary detention at Shaw Road
there was always one important and never-failing relief—working
on the Koran, reading and studying translations. Every day I
found it stimulating to read almost without a break. It was more
than a pleasant routine, it became a labour of love. The more
one reads the Koran, with translations and commentaries, the more
one learns. Reading through it again in my first study I got rather
excited at finding untold treasures. Studying a second time, newer
treasures came to light. When going through the Koran a third
time, inner meanings began to unfold themselves in quite familiar
passages. My fourth complete re-reading revealed again and again
more hidden jewels—happy rewards indeed!

Now I feel most deeply that my enforced detention proved to
be of the greatest benefit to me, if for no other reason than this,
that I had all the time in the world for this supreme study. It
was difficult to explain how great was the satisfaction, how warm
the pleasure I derived from these many hours with the Koran.
Only those who drink deep from this unending and refreshing
well can truly know and understand how profound and stimulating
the Holy Koran can be in its effect on the mind and heart. You
feel and know, as if for the very first time in your life, the real
meaning of soul—and especially your own.

IV. WEDDING INVITATION

WHILE I was thus passing my time, enduring the ever-lengthening days of waiting for freedom as happily and as best as I could under these encaged circumstances, a new development occurred. Although I did not know it then, once again, as so often before I was to go through the frustration of hopes rising high only to be dashed to disappointment!

One day in October a senior Special Branch officer came to see us. I mentioned in passing that my daughter, Rahmah, would be getting married in Penang in December, two months off. She was marrying Captain Mohamed Nizar bin Mohamed Zahari, of the Royal Malaysian Reconnaissance Regiment. He became interested at once, and said without any hesitation that if I wanted to go, arrangements could be made for me to attend the wedding. Naturally, this prospect made me feel very excited. I went round telling everyone I met I would be going to my daughter's wedding.

About two weeks later, I met another senior officer from Special Branch and told him about the wedding. I also asked a third officer, lower in seniority, to make it definite that I could go to the wedding. Foremost in my mind, of course, were the disappointments all three of us had suffered previously when our great expectations of going home were shattered. That is why I purposely told this officer I would very much appreciate it if the reply to my request to be present at the ceremony could come early, so that I would avoid having any last-minute disappointment, if for some reason my request was to be rejected. I simply felt I was not able to withstand the strain of any further period of dejection.

I should explain that a Malay wedding, following age-old customs, falls into two main parts—the *Nikah* and the *Bersanding*. To put it concisely, the *Nikah* is the marriage ceremony, the

Bersanding is the enthronement of the bride and groom, the bridal day. It is Malay custom that the bride and groom are King and Queen for a day! The custom goes back at least a thousand years.

The *Nikah* embraces and decides the legal formalities—agreement, endowment, and most important of all the consent and authority of the bride's father, who must be present. The *Nikah* is over in one day; the *Bersanding* with all its attendant rituals normally takes three days of feasting and celebration. In my case the *Nikah* ceremony had already been performed. This had taken place while I was in detention in The Special. I had been given two weeks' notice of the event. It occurred in March in the house of my brother-in-law, Wan Yahya, in Taiping in the presence of the Kathi there, and it was then that the wedding date had been set for December. A Kathi is a Malay learned in Islamic law.

Each week, whenever I went to the High Street Police Station to meet my family, I would eagerly remind the custodian A.S.P. to get me a reply. Imagine my feelings as a Malay father! I even made it clear that a refusal at the eleventh hour might cause heart-failure! I must say in all fairness that this officer appreciated my anxiety. At last—it was in November with little more than three weeks to go before the wedding day—my friend the custodian came to tell me that my request was granted—but there were several conditions. My heart rose; my face fell. The Ministry of Internal Security, he said, had decided that I should only be allowed to attend the *Bersanding*, and immediately it was over I would have to return to Kuala Lumpur. I would not be allowed to spend the night in Penang. My disappointment was so great that my eyes were wet as he was speaking. I would not be there for the two days before the *Bersanding*. I would not even be there to sit through the bridal night! I was so upset, my mind so far away, that I listened only formally to the other restrictions. He was talking about leave and costs. The other restrictions were that since I was asking for leave, which was not on compassionate grounds, (1) I would have to pay the cost of my trip to Penang and back, (2) I would be accompanied by police officers in plain clothes, and (3) They would not be allowed to claim mileage on their vehicles. In other words, I had to pay for their transport, too. I accepted all these conditions on the spot. I agreed automatically. There was no feeling of enthusiasm. I would have agreed to anything!

Now I realize why these conditions sounded so familiar to me. On three occasions, when I was a Minister and sought approval from the Prime Minister to visit various countries on duty, I was told I would have to pay for my transport myself. These duty-journeys related to favourite projects of mine. One was to build a urea fertilizer plant, the other to build a paper mill. How much I spent from my own money for these projects, I cannot remember! But I am deviating—that is another story. It is ironic to think of the great interest being taken now in fertilizers and paper mills—eleven years later!

Despite all the restrictions, at least I was allowed to go to my own daughter's wedding even if only for a day! I was relieved to learn that my family had not been told. I asked Special Branch to keep the matter confidential. I was too used to having my hopes crushed, so I did not want anyone in my family to endure this mental agony. One never knew—at the last moment Special Branch might change its mind! So I had to take any elation with caution, rather like noting the red warning on a bottle of medicine before drinking. Take care!

V. TASTE OF FREEDOM

NEXT day I felt better. In fact, I could hardly believe it. I was actually going to a wedding—and my own daughter's! I would be out at last, even if only for a short while! Anxiously I waited for confirmation. Please God, no change! The wedding date was 4 December. Just one week before the day. I learned once again about the actual arrangements being made. These proved to be better than those I had originally agreed to, even better than I could reasonably expect. First the officer assigned to accompany me said he did not want to be paid for his mileage, only for the cost of fuel and a little extra for the depreciation on his car. For this I was grateful, as it would reduce the total cost by two-thirds.

Even better news was coming my way! On the day before my actual departure for Penang, the custodian officer visited me again to say that I would be allowed to spend the night at home, and return on the next day! It seems to be normal for the Special Branch to act sometimes like a bargaining-counter, so as later on to demonstrate their great generosity! Nevertheless, I will always be grateful to God for whatever little bounty I did receive from the Special Branch during my period of detention.

Next morning, 4 December 1965, the great day dawned! Just before 6 a.m. we left Kuala Lumpur by road for Penang, 250 miles away. I was actually on my way! It couldn't be true! I was going home! The officer accompanying me owned a new Ford Cortina, which had hardly covered 1000 miles. By a curious coincidence I always seemed to travel in new cars owned by Special Branch officers–once during the journey after my arrest, and now when going back to Batu Maung on leave! Incidentally this man was a Chief Inspector of Police, promoted from Inspectorship, not being a gazetted officer or A.S.P., therefore he probably could not afford to buy a Volvo. He drove rather cautiously, and rightly so; he did not want to flog his car. Our drive proved uneventful, taking seven full hours to reach Butterworth.

We crossed over in the vehicle-ferry from Butterworth to Penang. There another Special Branch officer met me; he was taking over responsibility. I got into his car, together with one of my escorts from Kuala Lumpur, and so we drove on to Batu Maung. It was 1.30 p.m.; I was home at last!

After greeting my wife and family I learned that the Head of the Special Branch, Penang, Encik Baharom Shah bin Yahaya, and his wife had come to our home the previous day to inform my wife that I would be arriving from Kuala Lumpur at about 1 p.m. My wife and her brother, Wan Yahya, were both quite sceptical about the sincerity and genuineness of the visit by this officer, even though his wife was with him. In fact, my wife would not allow them to enter the house; she spoke to them from a window. But after Baharom Shah pleaded with her, claiming to be a distant relative, she relented and, on the advice of Wan Yahya, allowed them both to enter. So my wife knew the day before, but she kept it to herself.

Of course my home was alive with all the bustling activity that was normal during a wedding feast. There were hundreds of people already sitting down to lunch, and great activity going on everywhere inside the compound and also below the house where food was being served. When I suddenly arrived everything seemed to stop. It was a great surprise, quite unexpected. Guests left their seats in the middle of the feast, coming out to greet me. My wife, though very busy directing all the servers, hurried down accompanied by my aunts and uncles—only a handful of the elder generation still surviving.

There was joy everywhere. My wife was crying, but they were tears of joy. One by one my children came forward to kiss my hand. I noticed that they were trying to suppress their tears of happiness, but the tears still flowed. As for me, I was doing my best to maintain some kind of dignity. I did not want to show outwardly my overwhelming happiness, so I waved my hand to all the guests. Some of them came to kiss my hand, others embraced me.

As quickly as I could after this general welcome, I went upstairs to the main hall to join close friends and relatives in the feast. There I met for the first time my son-in-law's father, an Imam from a village near Ipoh, who was also a strong supporter of UMNO. Apart from all the guests who came to the wedding, all the villagers of Batu Maung turned up, whether invited or not. They wanted to welcome me and to show their regard for me personally, even though I was a detainee. Fortunately, there was food enough for everyone; my wife saw to that, as the Penghulu of the kampung had informed her they would all be coming, even without an invitation. After the feast, we found that our guests numbered nearly a thousand people.

I was delighted, of course. My pleasure was not shared by the Special Branch; I was told they were rather disappointed. They had expected the people of Batu Maung to boycott completely both me and my family! To lessen their disappointment, I told them that the presence of the kampung people in such great numbers was not because of me, but rather it was a tribute to my daughter, who taught their children in the local Sekolah Kebangsaan. This seemed to console some of the Special Branch officers in Kuala Lumpur.

By good luck, a former Muslim restaurant just below my home in the Garden Estate had been vacant for the past few months. The proprietor readily offered it to my wife to use for the feast. His generous action was doubly welcome as it saved us a great deal of money and labour. Without this facility, the family would have had to erect sheds and put up canvas tents in the compound for the wedding guests. Even our roof garden could seat about 150 people if it had a temporary weather-cover.

It is rare to have a reunion of all one's relatives at one time. In fact, ever since the death of my elder sister five years before, I had scarcely met any of my relatives from Perak and Kedah. Now, they were all present to show the solidarity and co-operation of the family during my absence in detention. Perhaps they also wanted to demonstrate that family sympathy and affection are stronger bonds than those of political beliefs. Many of my relatives belonged to the Alliance Party, yet they were all there to welcome me. Truly blood is thicker than water! Luckily for me, my relatives spared me unnecessarily tearful greetings—only a small number of elderly relations wept, especially my aunts; understandably, because aunts everywhere usually live in a different world from the present. I was fifty-one years old at the time of the wedding, so my aunts could not be less than sixty. Therefore, their tears were no surprise, since they were from the old world!

My police escort included one A.S.P. Special Branch officer, one D.P.C. from Kuala Lumpur, and another D.P.C. from Penang—all Malays. I invited them all to join in the feast, I ate my own wedding-lunch with relatives and close friends inside the house itself; the other guests dined in the restaurant below—the ladies on one floor, the men on another.

It turned out that the Penang Special Branch had sent two officers to see my brother-in-law, Wan Yahya, two days before, to tell him and also my wife that I would be coming to Batu Maung for the wedding, estimating my arrival time as 1.30 p.m. They also said I would have to leave on the same evening before midnight. In fact when I arrived, my family was not aware that new arrangements had been made—that I was allowed to stay that whole night at home. So this was indeed a very happy surprise for them; they were jubilant when I told them the news. Some relatives, however, had read speculations in the Press that I would be allowed leave for a few days, so they felt rather disappointed when they heard I could only stay just the one night. Even the villagers had expected me to stay longer. In fact, some came to the house to see me after I had left the next morning, and were rather disappointed.

It is hardly necessary for me to describe in detail the ceremonies that took place, as all Malay weddings are very much alike. There was one great difference on this wedding day. My brothers-in-law, in charge of the whole occasion, were rather strict about gate-crashers, particularly the Press—reporters and photographers alike. In fact, they had a few mild brushes with the Press, but they prevented them from getting access either to the house to report the wedding or to interview me. The Malay A.S.P. in charge was also very helpful. He allowed me to take my own time the next morning before I left for Kuala Lumpur. I did not actually go until 11 a.m., and even spent another half-an-hour shopping in Penang for such essentials as toilet requisites and shirts. Finally, at the ferry, they transferred me to the Ford Cortina.

This time my leave-taking was a far worse experience than when I was first arrested. The host of relatives present cried silently, but there was no moaning or wailing, which I do not think I would have been able to endure. For me it was a very sad farewell indeed. On the other hand, the great attendance at the wedding more than compensated for the sadness I felt as I left Penang once again, and for the continuing sense of loss that held my mind during the long and silent journey back to Kuala Lumpur. My deep dejection after my return was to hang over me like a heavy cloud for several days afterwards, in Shaw Road.

On the drive back we had lunch at a Muslim eating-shop in Kuala Kangsar. Once again people recognized me, both in the shop and outside, some even greeted me. They all knew about my going to my daughter's wedding, having read reports in the newspapers. It was night when we arrived in Kuala Lumpur. By 7.30 p.m. once again I was in custody. My taste of freedom was over!

I was, and will ever be, grateful to God for this great Mercy given to me, a memory to treasure always. Incidentally, one relative of mine who was at the wedding told me that when people in his Kuala Lumpur office read in the Press I was being given leave to attend the wedding, a few of his friends had wept in sympathy. May God bless them! I did not know it then, but later I heard news that left a very bitter taste in my mouth. I had no fear of anything that might happen to myself because of my faith in God. But why should others suffer merely because they felt kindly towards me? After the marriage, Special Branch officers questioned distant relatives and also adopted children of mine who had gone from Kuala Lumpur to Penang to attend the wedding ceremony. One of them was a former office-boy in *Utusan Melayu*, whom I had treated as my own son from the age of twelve. When questioned he was not afraid of any repercussions. Confidently, he spoke up in reply, 'Cik Aziz is like a father to me!'!

When I heard this, I told myself what a brave boy he was. But is there no limit to persecution? I had good reason to argue out this question with myself. It made me remember what had happened in Batu Maung after my arrest. UMNO Party leaders at all levels had not ceased to vilify me then. In the first month after my arrest, they held an UMNO seminar at Batu Maung, deliberately directing one of their loud-speakers towards my house. So deep was their spite against me, they even praised the Government for being generous in allowing my daughter Rahmah to continue working as a teacher, although her father was a traitor! And my wife and children had to listen to these voices of hate over the loud-speakers. Why should they have had to suffer this infliction, to hear such slander and malice pouring right into my own home?

VI. FRONT PAGE

Ever since I had been allowed outside our Jalan Shaw bungalow each morning to practise golf-shots, quite a number of people passing by recognized me. News of my presence there seemed to spread far and wide and rapidly throughout Kuala Lumpur. My own family actually did not know where my new residence was, as I always saw them at High Street, but soon they too heard where I was staying. On one visit to High Street, my wife whispered it to me. The Special Branch officer present smiled at her correct information, so I did not have to tell her myself. His smile saved me from breaking a very strict rule. My wife, thank God, is an observant woman! Soon I made it a kind of daily ritual to stay outside as long as possible, especially on mornings when one of my nephews would be going by in my father-in-law's car on his way to school, the Victoria Institution. At first he waved at me hesitantly, but later on his greeting grew more confident. He told his father and his uncles and aunts. They in turn passed the news to their friends or other relatives. My golf became quite a cheerful occasion. Each day people would wave to me as they sped by, even though I could not recognize them at a distance. But whether I knew them or not, I always waved back.

For nearly four months my right elbow had continued to give me pain. The doctors tried all kinds of drugs, but the relief proved only temporary. At one stage I could not even lift a cup to drink my tea. Finally, about three months before my release, our doctor suggested that I should be examined by an orthopaedist. I said I would prefer to have the State Orthopaedic Surgeon, Dr. Abdul Majid bin Ismail, examine me. Now a Tan Sri, the Director-General in the Ministry of Health, Dr. Majid was an old friend of mine. Arrangements were made for him to see me.

Before this, however, Special Branch officers, and even one

of our doctors, had asked me to stop playing golf, as this was causing my pain. I replied, 'Golf does not require any effort or strain by the right hand or elbow; it is the left hand which exerts the force. If a player strains his right hand or elbow, then his strokes are faulty.' I may not know medicine, but a keen learner knows his golf. Dr. Majid, who has a low golf handicap, being rated a good player, confirmed my comment. He suggested an injection between the bones of the elbow. Genuinely pleased to see me, he asked many questions. Of course, as a Special Branch officer was always present, right at my side, I could only tell him what I thought might be suitable for the Special Branch to hear and approve. Anyway, Dr. Majid generously gave me a few balls to supplement my rapidly depleting stock, as I used to lose them at the rate of three a week. This was not too bad, but when Datuk Raja began to be initiated into the mysteries of the game, the loss grew heavier, three balls a day. Later Datuk Raja used to receive golf balls from the Menteri Besar of Kelantan, Datuk Mohd. Asri, now a Cabinet Minister.

Dr. Majid next prescribed treatment by heat therapy for half an hour daily. So during the six weeks before my final release, my elbow was 'cooked' every day, except on Sundays and holidays. These treatments took place at the General Hospital. My visits would cause a considerable stir, evoking stares of surprise from the staff and visitors alike. Many came over to chat with me. Very few indeed showed no concern or sympathy for my well-being. Consequently my heat-treatments caused a lot of trouble to the very kind and considerate Special Branch officer who fetched me daily from Shaw Road to drive me to the Hospital and back. These hospital visits were rather like rehearsals for my debut on release, helping to put me back into public circulation by stages. At the hospital I met all kinds of people I used to know when I was a Cabinet Minister, and even from the years before my first election in 1955. So I had opportunities to assess their reactions to a detainee. Most were friendly, but others were non-commital in their remarks, just making small talk. One thing, however, became quite clear to me; so far no one had shown any contempt for me, or snubbed me. Almost everyone would ask after my health, even trying to study my face to see if it indicated that I had suffered much. A few ventured to ask if violence was the reason I was coming each day to the hospital!

Early one morning, when dawn was beginning to drive the night from the sky, I went out as usual to the football field near our bungalow. In the faint light, I could see a Morris Minor parked on the opposite side of the road. I also noticed that a man in the car had a camera, while another was walking towards the fence enclosing the field. It struck me at once—the Press was after me! When the photographer came closer I recognized him as being from the *Straits Times*. I shouted out, 'Go away!', and called a policeman to chase him off. He refused to go until the policeman threatened to arrest him. Then he went away, and so did the car. Being so engrossed in my game I soon forgot about the incident. Too late I realized that the car was moving slowly once more along the road. Looking up, I found a couple of men focusing their cameras on me. I signed to them to go away. They waved back, smiled, and then left. Why? Because they had already accomplished their mission. While I had been busy concentrating on my game during the previous ten minutes, they had already taken all the pictures they wanted.

I felt rather depressed when I realized what had happened, as ever since my detention began I had always been successful in avoiding the Press. During my many visits to the High Street Police Station to meet my family, the officers escorting me would always scout round to make sure no newspapermen were about. If any were, then they would take me to the interview room by a back door.

Later that morning I told my custodian A.S.P. about this incident with the Press, and asked him to use his official position to prevent the *Straits Times* from publishing my picture. He looked at me blandly, not seeming to show any anxiety or concern. Next day the *Straits Times* carried a report with four full-length pictures of me on the front page and inside. They claimed to have used tele-photo lenses. *Berita Harian* and the *Malay Mail* also printed large-size photographs of me. These news stories caused a lot of excitement in the next few days. About this time in 1965 continual wrangling was going on between the Malaysian and Singapore Governments on a multiplicity of subjects, each one arousing more rancour. One announcement said that Singapore would be releasing several Barisan Socialists from detention; their names were published. Bickering went on from both sides continually for almost two weeks. One day Encik Ishak remarked that all this quarrelling between the two Governments would benefit us, because we would become pawns in this game of rivalry, with each Government trying to out-smart the other, even on such a security question as the release of detainees. He was right!

VII. RELEASE?

RAMADAN, the Fasting Month, so precious to all Muslims, began on 5 January in 1966. During the third week of the fast, we were told one evening that we had to go to the High Street Police Station to meet some people there. No one explained why. As usual, I was the first to be sent. When I arrived, there were three Special Branch officers present, the ones whom we usually met. One was Raja Adnan, the Head of the Selangor Special Branch; another was Mr. Lim Suan Pong, the custodian A.S.P., and the third Encik Hashim Hassan, a senior journalist with Television and Radio Malaysia. In the room I found an impressive spread of cakes, sweets, coffee, tea and cigarettes laid out on a table. I did not have the slightest inkling of the reason for this get-together. Perhaps it concerned our release! Anyway, I was in no mood to be played about with, or to be tantalized once more, lest I should end up by being disappointed again. 'Once bitten, twice shy!', as the saying goes. Conversation was general—about my health, about the future of the Malays, about the weather, about business, or the cost of living. In fact they seemed to want to discuss almost everything under the sun, except the one subject most important to me—my release. So we wandered on and on for about one-and-a-half hours. When I left, feeling very disappointed about the whole party, my two co-detainees took my place to be entertained. Actually there was only time that day for one, for Ishak; the other, Datuk Raja, had his chat the next morning.

Strange as it may seem, they actually gave hints to my two friends (which they had not done with me) that the authorities were considering their release in the very near future. Would they be prepared to meet the Press and appear on T.V.? They replied that they had been badly let down on a previous occasion. Both Ishak and Datuk Raja had made Radio and T.V. confessions, yet nothing happened afterwards about an early release for them. Therefore they were not keen to go through a Press interview or appear on T.V. again, until they were certain they would be released. I can well imagine how embarrassed these senior Special Branch officers must have been to have two detainees speak to them in this manner. However, finally they did give them an undertaking, but they were also asked to keep the information dead secret. Naturally, when they came back to Jalan Shaw they were jubilant. Just as naturally, I was not. It struck me that perhaps my two friends would be released, but I would be sent somewhere else. However, my fears turned out to be unfounded. Next day the Chief of Selangor Special Branch came to inform me that moves were now being made to have all three of us released. He added that, if the arrangements did not fall through, we should be released before Hari Raya—the celebrations at the end of Ramadan. But—there was always a but—the whole affair was to be strictly confidential, lest something untoward should happen, and the proposed release be cancelled.

This officer also said I would be required to meet the Press and appear on T.V. I told him quite firmly that I would not answer any questions that would embarrass either me or the Government. I maintained that the statements I had given at my interrogations were the truth. 'Therefore,' I said, 'If I am questioned on any subject other than about my plans after my release, I will refuse to answer.' I did volunteer, however, to draft a statement regarding my intentions. He agreed. That afternoon I started working on a cockshy draft, which I sent next day to the Special Branch to be typed. Late that night I had doubts about the wisdom of using it. When I made the draft, it sounded good and quite sensible, but after sleeping on it overnight, my qualms increased. In the cold light of morning my draft tended to sound too boastful of my little efforts in the field of religion, both during my detention and before my arrest. On the other hand I could not let down the Special Branch officer, as I had promised him I would read out a statement. What to do? Nothing—just hope that it comes out all right, God willing!

I really could not spend any more time thinking about this draft, because suddenly I sat up all alert, every nerve tingling, my mind racing like the wind. My mirror showed me with the widest grin I ever had in my life. Thanks be to God! *I was going to be released*! I was so happy that I could not believe I was myself. I got up and dressed, chortling like a choir of minahs! I was jubilant at the prospect of spending Hari Raya at home—and Hari Raya was only ten days away! It was all too good to be true!

For the next few days nothing happened. We heard no more news or talk about any release. We were not even told what the conditions of our release might be. But, deep down somehow I had a feeling that this time it *would* take place. So I started to pack—my books, clothes, all my belongings, even finally looking around to make sure there was nothing left. I was all ready to go!

Three more days went by. Still no news. Four days—the same dead silence. Surely we were not to be left standing on the brink again? Was I right in thinking it was too good to be true? I was beginning to doubt the news very much. Then the fifth day dawned—six long days since the party at High Street, five since I had been told I would be released. What would it bring? The morning dragged on. At 2.30 p.m. an Assistant Superintendent of Police suddenly came in, obviously in a very great hurry. He told us he was instructed to talk about the conditions we had to observe when we were released. He was telling us about these token conditions to see if we would agree. Not having legal minds, we found the wording of these conditions seemed much less than we had anticipated. So we asked him for clarification. This A.S.P. was an Indian dressed expensively in civilian clothes, with boots lined with fur and a colourful shirt which could not have cost less than $50 at that time. His trousers were equally expensive. He tried to convince me by saying, 'We have had discussions for a considerable time among the senior officers so as not to make the conditions you will have to observe upon release too rigid.' 'As an example,' he said, 'we have waived one of the conditions, which normally would be a "must", that is having to report at the nearest Police Station where you reside at least once a week. Also, you are required to sign a personal bond of $500/-.'

Then he went on to say that he hoped we would accept the

following conditions; I quote the ones relating to me:

(1) That I will not leave the District of Balik Pulau, in which my house in Batu Maung is located, without the written permission of the O.C.P.D., Balik Pulau.

(2) That I will not leave the Island of Penang without first having permission in writing from the Chief Police Officer, Penang, and

(3) That I will not take an active part in politics or in trade union activities.

(4) That I was to give a personal bond of $500/- that I would not break these conditions.

My general reaction to these terms was not a happy one, as the whole question of conditions was only now being brought up. My two colleagues, Ishak and Datuk Raja, were ready to accept these conditions as they applied in their cases, I felt, however, that I should not accept them myself, as I was in a different category from my two fellow-detainees. However, both the psychological timing and the springing of a surprise at the eleventh hour, made me weaken my views. Willy-nilly I agreed in silence. Then he said he would prepare the Order of Release for approval by the Ministry of Internal Security. That day was Monday, 17 January 1966. Optimistically we hoped that we would be released soon—perhaps that same evening, or at least the next morning. Nothing happened that day. Nor on the following day. We were all on tenterhooks. Could it be that Fate had not yet decided? Were we going to suffer further mental torture? These were truly days of great anxiety. They seemed to stretch into eternity, hours dragging, tick-tock, tick-tock, each minute like another note of doom.

The next day, 19 January, was a Wednesday. As it was customary for the Cabinet to meet each Wednesday, our minds seized on the event. Such was our state of suspense, always waiting and waiting for news, we made a wild guess that this Cabinet meeting was our final hope—perhaps they were deciding even now on our final release. The morning dragged by—nothing happened! By 2.30 p.m., when we had almost given up hope that this would be *the day*, we decided to relax. The tension of the past few days was too much for us. Suddenly the Selangor Chief of the Special Branch entered saying, 'You are now free men. Will you get ready quickly and come with me?' He added that he was taking us in his car to Film Negara for a Press and T.V. interview. We learned from him that the Cabinet meeting that day had been unusually long; it did not finish until 2 p.m. So we had been correct after all in our wild forecast that a decision on our release was being made by Cabinet that day! While we were driving in the car I told the Special Branch Chief that on second thoughts I did not want to make the statement I had prepared earlier, as it tended to sound rather pompous. He gave me a look of surprise. I said I would merely say a few words about my intentions for the future, and no more. He then indicated that he was satisfied, as long as I did not say anything likely to embarrass the Government. However, he would warn the Press and T.V. personnel that I would not be taking part in the interview with my two friends. 'At last,' I thought, 'the Day of Release has come!'

VIII. PRESS CONFERENCE

WHEN we arrived at Film Negara, a battery of photographers trained their cameras on us. A host of Government Press officers and local and foreign correspondents sat waiting for us there. We went on to the luxurious office of the Head of Film Negara, Encik Mohd. Zain, where we had to wait for over forty minutes—while the studio was made ready, so we were told. Meanwhile, I cracked jokes with some Press Officers and newsmen; I knew them from my own days as either a journalist or a Minister.

What we did not realize then was the reason why we were in this office for so long. I found out why only the next day when I read the newspapers. While we were waiting, next door the Secretary-General of the Ministry of Information, Syed Zainal Abidin, was giving a Press Conference of his own.

According to the *Straits Times* report, he said:

'These men were detained because they were pursuing political objectives which led them to enter into a conspiracy with Indonesian agents. They were paid large sums of money to carry out instructions from Jakarta. They were obvious security risks. . .!'

When the three of us finally entered the Conference Room, I was asked to speak first. I made a very brief statement, as I had originally intended to do. I began my remarks with these words: 'This is the first time I have opened my mouth since my detention. I have only a few words to say. I have decided to give up politics for some years to come. This is a voluntary decision. I will be concentrating on religion. I began to take an interest in religion, my own type of religion, some four years back. Of course, I also have a lot of material for books which I will take my own time to write. There is no hurry. I can write on my own detention, but I don't know whether I can publish it; I know there is a good market. As a writer myself, I don't like to tell the Press what it is all about; I want to write it myself.' (Now I am writing it.)

The Press must have felt disappointed. Obviously they expected me to make some revelation. They did not get it, I then left the main table and took a seat in the audience among the reporters. Then the interview of my two co-detainees commenced.

The following report is from the *Straits Times* of 20 January:

'The former Socialist Front leader, Encik Ishak, began:

'I am overwhelmed. I can't express my happiness in so short a time. I am going back to be with my wife and children. The Government has treated me very well.'

A question and answer session followed. It went like this:

Q. Did you discuss your decision to quit politics with your former party colleague, Encik Ahmad Boestamam?

A. No, I was not in contact with him.

Q. What are your future plans?

A. My needs are simple and limited. First, I intend to concentrate on writing.

Q. Why did you decide to quit politics?

A. I think it is rather late in the day at my age [he is sixty] to go into active politics. After watching the political situation and mixing with people, I have come to the conclusion that politics is not very profitable.

Q. Do you think Socialism has a bright future in Malaysia?

A. It is not for me to decide. It is the people's problem.

Q. Have you cut off all your ties with the Socialist Front?

A. Yes, I have.

Q. Were you treated well by the Government?

A. Yes, we were given a good, quiet place to stay. We had television and radio, apart from books, newspapers and magazines to spend our time. While the other two played golf, I did gardening. Doctors visited us twice a week.

Q. Would you compare political detention in Indonesia with Malaysia?

A. I don't have the experience of having been detained in Indonesia.

Q. Did you expect to be released today?

A.   I was hoping to be released every day.

Encik Ishak also said he still believed in Socialism because of 'my up-bringing and family background'.

'There is no harm in believing in Socialism. I was detained because of my actions,' he said.

FORGET PAST

Again he was asked to comment on the political situation in Indonesia. He replied: 'Why ask about Indonesia alone? Why don't we discuss India, Pakistan and the peace bids in Vietnam?'

Q.   Why did you decide to set up a Government-in-exile instead of fighting out the issue here?

A.   Let us forget about the past and think of our future. I am not prepared to discuss things of the past.

Datuk Raja Abu Hanifah also declined to speak about the past. He added: 'Politics is in my blood, but . . . .' He did not elaborate.

Before the trio were brought into the conference room Syed Zainal said: 'These men were detained because they were pursuing political objectives which led them to enter into conspiracy with Indonesian agents.

'They were paid large sums of money to carry out instructions from Jakarta. They were obvious security risks and had to be prevented from carrying out their plot.

'Although they were taken into custody for indulging in acts amounting to treason, they were not subjected to any punitive measures.

'It was obvious at the time of their detention that they were under varying degrees of mental strain and confusion.

'Their detention gave them the opportunity for quiet reflection not only on their own personal positions but also on the political situation in the area.

'They have all reversed their political thinking to the extent that they are no longer considered security risks.

'One of them has in fact thanked the Government for detaining him before he reached the point of no return, and for giving him a chance to come to a more intelligent and sober analysis of the situation.

NO FUTURE

'These men have now voluntarily come to the conclusion that

they have no future in local politics and have decided to retire from active politics.

'In any case, one of the conditions of their release is that they should not indulge in politics.

'These men could have been released from detention earlier but for the fact that there was a definite threat to their lives and well-being if they were deprived of protection.'

At the end of the Press Conference, a Special Branch officer was heard telling Encik Aziz that he could leave for Penang, to rejoin his family.

I did not sit with the audience for very long, only about fifteen minutes; then I was taken back to the Film Negara Office, where I was left alone. There my custodian A.S.P., Mr. Lim, tried to contact my father at Gombak where he was staying, but failed to get him. Later on he told me my father was at the airport seeing off my brother-in-law, Dr. Johan Thambu, who was leaving for the United Kingdom to take a post-graduate course. A.S.P. Lim also tried to book an air passage for me to Penang so that I could rejoin my family, but the aircraft departure was much too early. I should not be able to make it in time. As an alternative Mr. Lim contacted the Railway Station but also failed to get a sleeper for me. As a result of these disappointments, I felt rather depressed. I then asked if he would be kind enough to take me to my father-in-law's house in Jalan Treacher, next to the Hotel Merlin. He agreed. From Lornie Road, where the Film Negara premises were then located, Mr. Lim drove me to the railway station to see if there had been any cancellation of sleeper bookings to Penang. The booking clerk was a young man who obviously had a high regard for me. He had heard over Radio Malaya that I was free, so he greeted me with a show of affection. I asked if there were any cancellations. He replied that there were none, but as two berths normally reserved for V.I.P.s had not been taken up, he would allot me one. 'After all,' he smiled, 'you are very much a V.I.P.'

Thanking him, I left for the Shaw Road bungalow to collect my belongings and discovered that both Ishak and Datuk Raja had already been there, and left. Without waiting for me to return, each had gone his own way—Ishak back to Ulu Langat in Selangor, and Datuk Raja to Seremban, both to their wives and families. As I looked round the 'home' I was leaving, I suddenly felt very lonely.

From Shaw Road we went to the house of my father-in-law, Wan Pawan Teh, who greeted me none too enthusiastically. Being an old-timer, a former M.C.S. (Malayan Civil Service) officer under the British, he felt perhaps that I was guilty of what I was charged with. Months later, he came to realise that all the allegations against me used by the propaganda machinery of the Alliance, were unfair. However, after greeting him, my sister-in-law, my nephews and a niece who was living there, I asked Mr. Lim to take me to Gombak Setia. My father was living there with my sister, three of my nieces and one nephew, all of them orphans. He had heard over the radio of my release on his return from the airport, so he was very happy indeed to see me looking well. He insisted I should stay to dinner, which I did, after performing the *Isha* prayer.

While I was at my father's house my brother, Encik Yusof, President of the Republic of Singapore, telephoned; he too, had heard the news.

After my *Isha* prayer my father's chauffeur drove me from Gombak to the station. As my son Zakaria was away from Kuala Lumpur, once again I felt rather neglected, having to go to the station without the company of anyone I knew very well. I would have an hour-long wait there before the train left. But, to my great relief, my old friend Encik Wahi Annuar was at the station. Also a former detainee, he had joined me as my Special Private Secretary in the Ministry of Agriculture, after having been rejected on his rehabilitation by all the other Ministries. I felt so happy, delighted that, thank God! I was not entirely forgotten. During the train journey my mind went back to those who were still in detention, among whom was Dr. Burhanuddin El-Helmy, the President of the Pan-Malayan Islamic Party who was detained one day earlier together with Datuk Kampo Radjo. His detention lasted two years, and he was not privileged enough to be sent to The Special. I was later informed that he completely denied the alleged plotting to set up a Malayan Government in Exile. Beyond this consistent denial he did not want to offer any further information, for which he was confined to his No. 1 cell. Later, he developed a serious urinary condition as a result of being denied permission to leave his cell as often as his bladder condition required him to. Although some years later the Government arranged for him to go to Australia for an operation, he died in 1968 after a lingering illness which perhaps was caused by this condition.

I saw him two weeks before he passed away, when in a faint voice he asked if the Indonesia-Raya concept or the Islamic form of Government would be somewhere near. 'God willing, it will come about', I replied.

IX. HOME AGAIN

NEXT morning after a lonely and restless night I arrived in Penang. It was 8.30 a.m. and I quickly hailed a taxi to hasten home to Batu Maung. Before getting into the taxi, however, I bought a copy of the *Straits Times* but I did not look at it. I tucked it away in my briefcase. I could only think of home—going home. Except for my wife and children no one knew what time I would be arriving home. The news of my release was on T.V. while I was on the train. I had asked my father to telephone to my good neighbour, Min Thau, that I would be on the Night Mail coming back to Penang. Later I found out this message had not been received by my wife, as Min Thau and his wife were in town, away from home. My wife learned from the Police that I had left Kuala Lumpur.

Home at last! When my taxi arrived there was my wife waiting for me alone at the gate. It was a quiet, but very happy reunion. Both my daughters, Raziah and Umi, were still in school, so except for my wife there was no one else of my own family to greet me. I could not care less; I was too glad to be home and with my wife again. Never has my home looked better; everything was in its place. My old rosewood Chinese settee with eight chairs and four side-tables, complete with offertory tables, looked older than its 150 years, shining more brightly than I had ever known. The sea, too, was glistening with sunshine. As it was Sunday, the waters were dotted with holiday-makers skiing. I did not say much, my feelings were too deep for words, but a silent prayer of gratitude to God seemed to murmur with every beating of my pulse, repeating—Allahamdullilah, Allah be Praised! I sat with my wife in the lounge overlooking the southern approaches to Penang Harbour and occasional ships passing by. It was good to be savouring once more this scene well-known to me, a picture I had often

recalled with fond memory during the many months I was languishing in detention. It was no longer a vision in the mind—I
was seeing it with my own eyes! Neither did my wife say much,
at least not for some time. She merely mentioned that my youngest
girl Umi had been training hard for her school sports, which would
be taking place in about ten days. Really there was no need for
either of us to talk, the satisfaction of being home again was
enough—to be together after such a long, long time.

The people of Batu Maung knew I had been released, but they
did not know when I would be returning home, so my taxi passing
through the village at the foot of the hill below my house created
quite a stir, but they could only wave after the taxi passed by.

That afternoon a few of the village elders called to welcome
me home—a genuine sentiment indeed, as it happened that we
were in the fasting month again. Normally, this being so, none
would have come. All were truly happy to see me despite the
continuous propaganda they had heard blackguarding me ever
since I was arrested. Apparently the propagandists considered I
was the greatest villain in the country, a traitor to my nation
and people. But propaganda does not have to be believed merely
because it is heard. Strange as it might seem to those responsible
for slanders against me, two days after I arrived home these same
elders, together with the Headmaster of the Batu Maung National
School, came to ask me to officiate at the school's annual sports
meeting one week later and to give away the prizes. This was
the school where my daughter Rahmah had taught after leaving
College. While I was in detention she had been transferred to
Johore Bahru so that she could be with her husband, who was
stationed with his army unit in Singapore.

After my noon prayers I started to look at the daily papers
and the report in the *Straits Times* of our release, complete with
pictures. Then I read for the first time the statement by Syed
Zainal Abidin made at the secret Press Conference. Astounded,
I felt rather bitter about the duplicity of either the Special Branch
or the Government. The Selangor Chief of Special Branch had
not told me of their plan that Syed Zainal was to make an adverse
statement about me. If I had known I would certainly have denied
it to the Press on the spot, and thus willy-nilly have caused con-

siderable embarrassment to the Government. Then, I thought, it was just as well I did not know—perhaps I might have been detained again!

It did, however, seem very strange indeed that the Government even at this stage still wanted to pursue me with allegations which they knew only too well had no foundation. Immediately I telephoned the Head of Penang Special Branch, telling him of my dumbfounded surprise on reading the statement by Syed Zainal. I asked him to convey a strong protest from me to the Special Branch Headquarters in Kuala Lumpur, seeking a correction in the Press saying that I was not included in the 'trio' who had received large sums of money. Syed Zainal, some years later, died a gruesome death in a car accident in Kuala Lumpur.

At no time—either before, during or after my detention—would the Special Branch say that I had received money from Indonesia, or from Indonesian agents. They knew very well the accusation was false, and yet they were a party to spreading this untrue charge.

A few days later, about a week after my return, I received a letter, which was addressed to my former home in Morib, and had been re-directed to me at Batu Maung. On opening it, I almost jumped with joy. It was the first letter of encouragement and sympathy I had received since my return home. Happily, I read:

My Dear Aziz,
  I was delighted to hear of the change in your fortunes which has taken place and I trust you are none the worse for your enforced holiday.
  I shall look forward to reading your book.
  I take this opportunity of sending you all good wishes for the present season.
                    With kindest regards,

                                            Yours sincerely,

I could not read the signature, but it was familiar indeed, and the letterhead told me whose it was. The letterhead was 'Lord President's Chambers, The Federal Court, Kuala Lumpur'. The author was Sir James Thomson, the Lord President, a man whom all admired and respected. I received this kind and courteous note on 28 January and I replied:

2nd February, 1966.

My Dear Sir James,

Thank you very much for your kind letter which I received a few days ago, it having been redirected to Penang.

My enforced holiday, as you called it, has been in some ways a blessing. For one thing, I have come to realise what true values are in this everyday life. You, especially, will appreciate that there can never be a restoration of true values nor true justice for anyone with a higher purpose in life.

I am afraid I still have to think again about writing my second biography covering the period as a member of the Alliance Government. The book if written, will inevitably be an embarrassment to some of my former friends and colleagues.

Finally, my wife joins me in wishing you and Lady Thomson the very best. I remember Lady Thomson very well, especially during the UNFAO Regional Conference in Kuala Lumpur just before my retirement.

With kindest regards,

Yours sincerely,
ABDUL AZIZ ISHAK

'Well,' I thought, 'how wonderful it was of Sir James to write so soon to me. He must have done it straight after reading the morning paper, as soon as he reached his office.' It was a nice feeling to have in the midst of my worries about the falseness of the published statement in the papers that the head of the highest Court in the land wished me well!

A little later, a second letter came, from another man learned in the law—Mr. Justice Mohamed Suffian (now a Tun and also Lord President). I had been good friends with him and his wife ever since the end of World War II. In his letter Mr. Justice Suffian said he was very happy to hear the news and wished me all good fortune now that I was released. He went on to pen an open invitation to drop into his home in Kuala Lumpur at any time. Perhaps we would discuss the breeding of orchids. He and his wife were very keen on trying to produce new hybrids. So his warm sympathy and encouragement added to my cup of joy. At that happy moment I was not to know that the cup would be broken many times before I could call myself a free man again.

X. PISTOL-POINT

THREE days after the Fasting Month ended, a senior police officer at Headquarters, whom I knew very well, came to my house in Batu Maung, accompanied by the Head of Special Branch, Penang.

'Has anything been done about my protest?' I asked at once. I said, 'I have no intention of actually taking up the issue with the Government, but if Syed Zainal will make a correction to indicate that I was not included in the 'trio' who received money from Indonesia, I will be satisfied.' Alternatively, if he did not, I added, I would have no choice but to resort to legal action against Syed Zainal personally and against the *Straits Times* for publishing the story. The officer seemed to be in a dilemma, but he realized on which side his bread was buttered! He tried to reassure me, saying he knew nothing about it at all, that he would go back to Kuala Lumpur and try to get my request met. His excuses all sounded rather thin to me.

I told them both about my grave financial position. I owed the Malayan Finance Corporation $30,000/-; my overdraft with my bank was $5,000/- plus interest. I also owed the Income Tax Department about $2,000/-, and various sundry debtors another $3,000/-. In fact when I was detained I had hoped that some friends would pay off the interest on the loans from the Finance Company and the bank, but they were not able to do so for very long. They did pay for the first few months, but then allowed them to lapse. Reasonable enough—it would be too much for me to expect them to pay for an indefinite period. Then I informed these Special Branch officers that during the 1959 elections I had found a quick way of making money by writing my biography. It had taken me two months to finish, but the proceeds from sales helped to pay some of my election debts. If the book distributors paid in full, I would have been quite well off financially, even now.

Therefore I wanted to write once again as a matter of urgency—first the story of my detention, and after that the second part of my biography, covering the period when I was in the Alliance Government. When both these were completed I would, I hoped, have earned more than enough to pay my outstanding debts. 'The first book on my detention will find a ready market outside the country,' I said. Then I outlined the kind of material I would be including in the story of my detention. They were taken aback, horrified that they and their colleagues would be featured in a book. So they suddenly seemed to become very anxious to assist me in whatever way they could to relieve my financial plight, and thus hope to prevent me from writing such a book, which could be, to say the least, quite revealing.

'I don't want any postponements,' I said, 'as I wish to solve my financial problem outright by writing these two books. I know no other way of earning my living.'

I also told them that soon after I broke with the Alliance Government in 1963, various friends and well-wishers had invited me to go into business. One was a well-known personality in insurance. He wanted me to head a new company on an international basis. After a great deal of groundwork had been done, the original sponsors, all wealthy businessmen, were dissuaded—so I learned later—from giving their support to the project, as it was associated with me. This was to be expected; I felt more sorry than disappointed. Later, a group of Singapore friends, former schoolmates of mine, planned to start a Singapore Government project processing garbage from the City Council areas in Singapore into compost. Considerable research had already been done. Negotiations went on for more than a year. At that time, late 1963, Singapore had just become a State in the new Malaysia. Finally my brother, Encik Rahim Ishak, went to see the Prime Minister, Mr. Lee Kuan Yew, to tell him about my taking part in the project. Mr. Lee agreed—after having checked the records of my friends and finding them non-politically inclined. He also mentioned that as he was soon going to Kuala Lumpur from Singapore he would inform the Prime Minister of Malaysia, Tunku Abdul Rahman.

A few weeks later someone asked me, 'If you were in Tunku

Abdul Rahman's position would you agree to allow a dangerous member of the Opposition to be financially strong enough to continue to oppose him?' That was the end of my efforts to go into business after my break with the Alliance, and leaving the Cabinet, as my friends and co-sponsors in the garbage project withdrew. Ironically, that is for me, the plant did get constructed in 1972, and who provided part of the share capital as a loan to the operators—the Government of the Republic of Singapore.

I told both these experiences of mine in 1963 to the Special Branch officers. I also informed them of what happened to me as a writer in 1964 after I had moved from my home in Morib to Batu Maung following the elections that year, which I did not contest. At that time, I had ready the manuscripts for two books, both on travel. Having no money as capital I went around hawking these MSS. with publishing companies in Penang. All politely told me that they could not afford to risk the Government's displeasure by publishing my books. I made no further effort after that impasse. It seemed that I had no other alternative but to earn a livelihood through the kindness of the Alliance Government. This, of course, I would not do. If I had wanted to, I would not have left the Cabinet. I need not have left, as Tunku Abdul Rahman wanted to transfer me to another Ministry, but I declined.

Then I brought my talk with these Special Branch officers back to the question of my detention. I said, 'The books I have in mind to produce on this theme will be so topical and exciting that I feel certain I will be able to publish them whether in Malaysia or overseas. As you can see my financial plight is desperate!'

They asked me, however, not to do anything until I heard from them. I agreed. Meanwhile, I sent a cable to my brother-in-law, Encik Wan Suleiman, then Solicitor-General. I asked if he could spare a weekend to come up to Penang, as I needed legal advice very urgently. He called me back the same day, saying he was extremely sorry, but he could not assist me, as in his official capacity he was adviser to the Ministry of Internal Security and to the Government generally. He gave me the name of a well-known lawyer in Penang, asked me to see him, and to mention that he had sent me. Without much delay I telephoned this lawyer—I do not name him—to make an appointment. When we met, I gave him a brief introduction to my problems. After listening, he said at the very outset that he was unable to assist me, as he supported the Government and was also a personal friend of Tunku Abdul Rahman. However, he advised me not to precipitate events which would inevitably lead me to a second detention. He told me frankly that for the time being I had no means of redress; I could not challenge the Internal Security Act. I thanked him for his frankness and sincerity, and left.

For more than a week I heard nothing further from Special Branch, until one day I happened to go to Penang. There I telephoned the Head of Special Branch, who suggested that we should meet in his office. He said he had no further information, but he would be going to Kuala Lumpur the next day and would ask for a reply to my earlier requests. I told him about my telephone conversation with Wan Suleiman and my meeting with the lawyer. This information seemed to excite him. His Deputy was present during this conversation. Then I said I wished to go to Singapore to see my daughter, Rahmah, whom I had not met since my release. He asked me to apply in writing, and in the meantime he would also mention this at the Kuala Lumpur Headquarters. He suggested my request could be met if I were to report certain things that might be useful to our Government while I was in Singapore. He did not specify what. Without hesitation I told both him and his Deputy that I would not consent to doing work of that kind, and I had never done so before. Quickly he changed the subject. I could not really blame him for making this improper suggestion; to him it would seem quite in order. After all, he was doing a job, earning his living.

A few days later he returned from Kuala Lumpur and came to see me at Batu Maung. I was now feeling rather cautious about him. I reminded myself that the only real sincerity of most people is with God. But I knew that he, like me, was a God-fearing man of some years' standing. Therefore we should be able to discuss Muslim theology in its application to everyday life, particularly my present problem. We did so. On the question of my plight, he gave his spiritual version of my seeking need. Likewise, too, he considered my other problem, that of earning an honest living in the way I was accustomed to—by writing. The replies he gave me were simply echoes, identical to those I had heard from the lawyer. A coincidence? I wonder. If anything, he was more positive. According to him the authorities would not hesitate to arrest me again if I persisted in doing anything that would bring the Government into disrepute when writing my biography. I would be treated likewise in regard to my other book on my arrest and detention. As neither of his answers could help in the problem of earning an honest living, I replied, 'Well, the only alternative I have left is to declare myself a bankrupt.'

I elaborated on this theme. During my public examination for bankruptcy, I said, it would be inevitable that I would have to reveal all the difficulties I encountered since I decided I did not want to continue as a Minister in the Alliance Government.

I realised then that to survive I must not allow my faith to be shaken by this brick-wall attitude of the Government. I had been detained. Now I was released, but I was not free. I was subject to restrictions, which obviously the authorities intended to enforce. And how long this state of affairs would last I did not know. 'My only Protector is Him!', I thought, 'I have no other Protector! I have to submit my will to His Will; and in doing so I hope to be accepted as a true Muslim.' On further reflection, I said to myself, 'I cannot continue forever living at pistol-point!'

PART III

Bear not false witness: let the lie
Have time on its own wings to fly.

ARTHUR HUGH CLOUGH, *The Latest Decalogue*

I. UNDER WATCH

IT was now March. I had been home again for one month. I felt strongly that I must see Rahmah in Singapore. She was teaching at an English school in Johore Bahru. So I applied to go to Singapore. The Special Branch told me that I could not go there, but I could go anywhere else in Malaysia. So I decided to see her in Johore Bahru. On the day before I left on my way to meet her, the Special Branch said I could go only to Kuala Lumpur, and not to Johore Bahru.

So, when I arrived in the capital I contacted a senior Special Branch officer I used to know, telling him of my disappointment at not being allowed to go to Johore Bahru. I also mentioned that I had with me some of my daughter's clothes, as well as some cakes her mother had taken the trouble to prepare for her. He answered, 'I cannot help you.' When I pointed out that I had not seen her since my release, he replied that he would make arrangements for her to come and see me in Kuala Lumpur instead.

Next morning I was surprised when my son-in-law, Captain Mohamed Nizar, telephoned from Singapore asking why the Special Branch required Rahmah in Kuala Lumpur during the next couple of days. Apparently two Special Branch officers in Johore Bahru had gone to the school where my daughter was teaching and told the Headmistress that Rahmah was required to go to Kuala Lumpur immediately. The reason they gave was that I wanted to see her. Naturally she wanted to know the true reason so that Rahmah could be given leave on compassionate grounds. But since the Special Branch officer did not specify any reason, therefore she had to classify Rahmah's leave as 'not on compassionate grounds'. In other words, Rahmah would have to go to Kuala Lumpur on no-pay leave!

These Special Branch officers did not see my daughter personally to explain to her the true reason. So when her husband spoke to me, I asked him to ignore the request from Special Branch and to tell Rahmah not to come to Kuala Lumpur at all. Oh, what officials could do to mess things up!

Later I telephoned the senior Special Branch officer in Kuala Lumpur H.Q. to complain about the methods used by his officers to intimidate my daughter into going to Kuala Lumpur without telling her the real reason for the trip. 'It is a typical example of the misuse of power', I said. 'Such conduct tends to discredit and bring into disrepute the good name of Special Branch.'

As I could not go any further than Kuala Lumpur, I stayed for only five days before returning to Penang. But I did not let my dejection over the failure to see my own daughter prevent me from taking whatever further action was possible.

I made arrangements to meet the senior Special Branch officer at Headquarters in Bluff Road. After a few days, he came to my father-in-law's house at Treacher Road, accompanied by the O.C. Special Branch, Selangor. My idea in having this meeting was to tell him how I was being systematically intimidated by his men, directly and indirectly. I had received several visits from people whom I knew to be his agents. One of them was actually a nephew-in-law of mine. He had come to see me with the double motive of visiting me and also getting information about my general attitude and trends of thought. His wife was with him. After pretending to tell him a great deal, I then warned him as a relative not to sell himself cheaply as an informer or a spy.

'The present low status of the Malays in our own country,' I said, 'is partly due to people like you—Malays who are ready to become informers or act as agents just for the sake of money. In any country such people are despised as traitors. The Prophet warned against men like you. I am sorry to have to say this to a relative—but it is for your own good.'

I told these Special Branch officers that they had sent along agents who pretended to be friendly to me, offering their services in helping with my autobiography, by typing, polishing-up, etc. I had responded to their overtures, but I did not trust them. They stopped coming, when they found out, after several such visits, that I was not likely to let them have even a peek at my manuscript.

But one day in August 1966 my brother, Rahim, who was by then the Minister of State for Education in the Singapore Government, came to stay at Batu Maung for a few days. This was at the height of active confrontation between Malaysia and Singapore after their separation. Two Special Branch agents came to my house again. They had someone else in their car, a man I recognized as having previously been in the vicinity of my home operating a walkie-talkie. But when they discovered that Rahim's car was not in my compound, they immediately left, telling my wife that they were rather busy. I strongly suspect that their intention on this occasion was to be introduced to Rahim in the hope that they might be able to get some information out of him during a conversation. Little did they know my brother! Or me!

'Stop sending such people,' I said. 'It is an insult to my intelligence.'

They denied strongly that they were responsible, although they seemed to know the persons to whom I was referring. I also said I had information that the Government wanted to try and trap me again, to get me detained a second time. This was the reason for sending so many strangers to my house to masquerade as would-be friends and sympathizers.

'Stop sending such people to me. If it is your intention to detain me again, well then—get on with it!' I said. 'I cannot bear continually to be kept in a state of tension by visits from such unrefined and amateurish agents and informers, whose only purpose is to report their assessments of the workings of my mind.'

In reply, these officers wanted to know the name of the person who informed me that it was the Government's intention to detain me again. I refused to give a name. Then one of these officers, a man of religious turn of mind, started to pacify me by referring to some Koranic sayings. So our meeting ended. I felt certain they were rather taken aback by my general attitude.

In the month of May my daughter Rahmah was admitted to Johore Bahru Hospital as a patient, but she had been there nearly two weeks before I heard about it. Immediately I informed the O.C. Special Branch, Penang, that I wanted to go to Johore Bahru to see her. Next day, the local police told me she had been discharged from hospital the previous day, but if I still wanted to see her in Johore Bahru I could have permission. Without hesitation, I said I would go.

Next day when the same policeman came to confirm the date and time of my departure from Penang, I said that after careful consideration I had changed my mind. In the first place my daughter lived in Singapore; if I wanted to see her, I could do so only briefly at her school in Johore Bahru. In any event she would be coming to Penang during the school holidays in less than a month. I learned later that the Special Branch officers in Kuala Lumpur were very angry with me for playing the fool with them. They said at first I wanted to go, and after all the difficulties, the granting of permission and making other arrangements, I changed my mind. Of course, they had a right to be very angry, but I also had rights, even as an ex-detainee, to change my mind if I wanted to, especially on the very sound grounds that I could ill afford to go to Johore Bahru in my present financial straits.

My life in Batu Maung continued to be very dull. I seldom went into Penang Town. I arranged my visits to go there only twice a month. I would call at the Penang Library to change books and magazines, do some shopping, and then return home. Every Friday I attended the congregation at the local mosque, situated about a mile from my house. I enjoyed walking to the mosque and back, always carrying an umbrella, rain or shine. Apart from my Friday visits to this mosque, I used to enjoy kampung weddings. I was always invited, if there was one taking place anywhere in the district. I made a special effort to attend all funerals in the vicinity, happy to take part in the *sembahyang jenazah*, the prayer for the dead. I was a changed man. In all my earlier life I had never cared to go to funerals. Signs of growing old, I suppose.

My routine morning walk would usually be to the landing place at the foot of my hill to buy fish for the day. It was a place to remember. It was here that I had read the news of the overnight arrest of my co-detainees on the very day I had been later taken myself. This landing place caters not only for the local fishermen, but also for others who fish off Pangkor Island to the south or Kuala Kedah to the north. These fishermen would land a good haul, an average of between 50 and 100 piculs per boat, if they were operating a drag net. At times, however, a whole fleet of *Pukat Jerot* boats would return empty, not having come across any shoals of fish. On such days local people like myself would either buy fish from old-type handline-fishermen, or go without.

When fish are plentiful—either *chencharu* or *kembong*, *tongkol* or *selar*—local people can buy for thirty cents as much as three to five katties from the *Pukat Jerot* boats. These fish are much fresher than those to be bought anywhere else inland. Prawns, *sotong* and *ikan sisa nabi* or lemon sole, all highly-esteemed by good restaurants in Penang, sell at less than half the price at Batu Maung. They are caught by bag-nets fixed to the bottom of the sea in waters not more than fifteen feet deep.

For food generally, Batu Maung and the surrounding areas can be considered as cheap for living. We plant our own vegetables. We do not raise chickens for eggs or meat, as I object strongly to the smell in or around the house. To keep away unwelcome visitors at night, we rear a few geese, rather than keep dogs. They are reputed to scare away snakes of which there used to be many in our compound. Since we began raising geese, we had not seen a snake for months.

My home at Batu Maung had long been a subject of barrage propaganda by Tunku Abdul Rahman and other UMNO leaders. This was especially so at the time of my arrest and during my detention. They attacked my character mercilessly. I was accused of building my house on the rocks of Batu Maung at the edge of the sea with money received from Indonesia. Later I found out that people had actually believed this mischievous propaganda.

I did not become aware of this until about a year after my release from detention. That would be about February. It happened this way. I had attempted to do some business in mining for tin ore. Two of my associates, both Malays, came to stay with me at Batu Maung. After working closely with me for over a year they confessed that during their visit, they had tried in vain to find likely trap-doors near or under the built-up fish-ponds, which President Soekarno's submarines could enter and leave by underwater channels. Of course there was nothing of the kind. It was one of Tunku Abdul Rahman's flights of imagination, which viewers of such television programmes as 'Sea Voyage' could stretch to their limits by localizing their vicarious adventures. Most people like spy stories. Just imagine—if anyone found a submarine cave, Aziz Ishak would be a spy!

In 1971, five years after my release, I took Tunku Abdul Rahman on a trip from his house in Jalan Ayer Rajah in Penang to Batu Maung to show him my house as a prospective buyer. I was very broke. He came, examined the house, and was rather impressed. He told me he would buy it as a week-end holiday house after his term as Secretary-General of the Islamic Secretariat was over. When that time came, some four years later, he made a jovial hint about acquiring my home, but I was better off financially then, so I said with a laugh, 'It's not for sale now.' The Batu Maung house is still mine.

Incidentally—it is one of the strange coincidences of my life— my former official house at No. 1, Jalan Kenny, Kuala Lumpur, when I was one of his Ministers, is now the Tunku's official residence in the capital. In 1974 they renamed the road Jalan Tunku. The modest wooden home I built in Morib, Selangor, after I left my official house in Kuala Lumpur in 1963 was also sold. The buyer—Tunku Abdul Rahman. Strange as it may seem, house-wise Tunku Abdul Rahman has always been tracking me!

II. RESTRICTIONS

BEING a released detainee, bound to abide by restrictions on movements outside my own District, apart from specified activities such as politics or trade unions, life is not easy. 'I have to earn a living,' I thought, 'but being a writer, how am I to do so, if Special Branch is holding a threat of further detention over my head if I do? I sympathize with Damocles. I know his feelings of having a sword suspended by a thread hanging ready to fall on his head.' 'What is the use,' I reflected, 'of staying on here if I can't earn a living? Would it not be better to go away from Malaysia altogether, and live in Singapore? At least I will be my own man there. But how to get there?'

I decided it was worth trying, although I must admit at the time it was taking a long shot. However, perhaps the Government might welcome the chance to be rid of me. Well, there was no harm in asking.

Early in May I telephoned the Private Secretary to the Prime Minister, Tunku Abdul Rahman, to ask if he would give me an appointment to have a talk with him. I received an affirmative reply, and arranged to go down to Kuala Lumpur. In our conversation in his magnificent office I asked the Tunku if he would give me permission to leave Malaysia and go to live in Singapore. I also asked if the present restrictions applying to me could be withdrawn altogether. The Tunku told me quite amiably that there was nothing he could do about either request. A decision on both these matters was entirely within the judgement of Special Branch. I would have to apply to them.

While I was in Kuala Lumpur for three days, I spoke on the telephone several times with the Permanent Secretary of the Ministry of Home Affairs in relation to both these requests, asking for consideration by Special Branch.

I returned to Batu Maung. A month passed, but I had heard nothing. On 13 June I decided to send a telegram to the Permanent Secretary to stir up action. He replied at once by telegram as follows:

'RE YOUR TEL THIS MORNING MATTER UNDER CONSIDERATION STOP WILL WRITE SOONEST POSSIBLE.'

Another month without any further news! I was still getting the same treatment as when I was actually in detention. Always the same monotonous procedure—Telephone Request—Wait—No Reply—Telephone Again—Under Consideration—Wait—No Reply—Telephone Again. Wait again—and so it goes on and on.

I decided to write once more. On 12 July I sent the following letter to the Permanent Secretary, Ministry of Home Affairs:

'It is exactly one month since I received your telegram and yet no decision on my enquiry. It is useless for me to return to Kuala Lumpur.

'My present predicament and future well-being are very important to me. I shall therefore be grateful if the Minister could give his rulings on the various matters raised with you in May last.

'Pending a decision, I am arranging for my wife and family to spend the coming school holidays in Singapore with our daughter who teaches at an English School in Johore Bahru but lives in Singapore with her husband. It would be a happy gathering and reunion if I can also be able to go for two weeks. I am therefore seeking permission for the visit to commence about the 31st of this month.'

Finally, a reply came. Dated 16 July, it read as follows:

'Reference your letter of 12th July, 1966, in regard to your request to be allowed to move and reside in Singapore, I regret to inform you that no decision has yet been made by the Government in this matter. I shall immediately communicate with you as soon as a decision is made.

'With regard to your request for permission to visit for two weeks beginning from 31st July 1966 the Honourable the Minister of Home Affairs has allowed your request.'

Note that the reply is 'Yes' to the third request, the first is still being considered, and the second, on withdrawal of all restrictions, not mentioned at all.

The next phase was slightly different—silence at both ends. I was on the end of the queue, waiting again. How long would it last this time? Somewhat to my surprise, it came much more rapidly than I ever expected. The next missive from Kuala Lumpur was dated only five days later, 23 July, and from the same source, as follows:

> 'I refer to your letter of 12th July, 1966, in regard to your request to be allowed to move and reside in Singapore.
>
> I am directed to inform you with regret that the Government is not prepared to accede to this request.'

So that was that! At least I knew where I stood. Note that no mention is made whatever about withdrawing the restrictions, let alone relaxing any of them. I wondered why the Government refused my requests. The answer was very plain, it was so obvious. They were still afraid of what I might do, if either request was granted. Although I was released they were uncertain of me. If they agreed, perhaps I might settle down in Singapore, speak my mind freely about a number of matters. Worse still, I might even join the P.A.P.—the People's Action Party—under Prime Minister Lee Kuan Yew! After all my elder brother was President of the Republic, my younger brother Minister of State.

'How strange,' I thought. 'First I was detained because I was considered a security risk in relation to Indonesia's confrontation of Malaysia. Now apparently, even though released on restriction, I am considered a risk again in relation to Singapore.' It was clear to me now that although I was technically powerless, I was still a man they could not afford to let off the leash. It was also clear to me now that it would be useless to continue with any further requests, except of a minor nature. The answer would always be the same 'No'. In a very real sense, I was still under close surveillance, almost, I might say, still under detention. Quite a paradox!

III. ANOTHER ORDER

'Well, what now?' I thought. My two major requests are either rejected or ignored, but the minor one, comparatively speaking, was allowed. I could go to Singapore for the August holidays. So I decided I would. I had a family reason for going, but at the same time my presence in Singapore and my behaviour there would show the powers that be that I was quite sincere in my repeated claim. I did not wish to embarrass the Government.

The family reason was that my wife—who had already gone ahead of me—rang to say that my daughter, Rahmah, would be going into Johore Bahru Hospital to have her first child.

Off I set, prepared to stay two whole weeks in Singapore, to live in my daughter's house, rarely go out, and generally behave like a father and potential grandfather. I was quite happy indeed with this prospect of a family reunion, sure that these would be the first really carefree weeks I had spent since my release. But straight after I arrived, I had to rush off to the hospital with my son-in-law, Captain Mohamed Nizar. The baby had come!

He, of course, was just as excited as I was, probably more so seeing he was the father. It was a boy! My first grandson, a day to celebrate. I could not know then that the time would come when I would be a grandfather ten times over—eight of them boys! My elder brother, Yusof, President of the Republic of Singapore, held a private family party for all of us in the Istana (Government House).

After this happy family holiday, I returned to Batu Maung. If the Special Branch had been keeping an eye on all my movements in Singapore, surely they must have been satisfied then that I was a man of my word.

It was now mid-August. I resumed my daily routine—prayers, walks, golf, occasional visits to town. It was a vegetating period, as I had no real purpose in life. How could I? I could not work at my profession without eyes peering over my shoulder. I was filling in time day after day.

To my astonishment I received a letter out of the blue from the Ministry of Home Affairs at the end of August. This message stated that the Government had given some further consideration to my earlier requests, and were prepared to 'allow me to move to and reside in Johore' if I so wished.

On 2 September I replied saying that no such request had ever been made by me. I had asked to go to Singapore. I stated that the idea of Johore had originated from the Prime Minister, who had suggested it as a possibility when I had seen him the previous May. I had rejected it then, and was now doing so again. I pointed out that it was rather pointless, and certainly economically unreal, for me to be put to the expense of setting up a new household in Johore, when I already had a home of my own in Penang. Moving to Singapore would involve no economic hardship for me—I had enough financial troubles as it was—because I could stay there either with my daughter or my relatives. That will be the last I will hear from the Ministry, I reflected. I can lead a peaceful life in and around Batu Maung. There will be no more worries and frustrations coming to me, I hoped. I was resigned to my fate; the future, as always, is an unknown sea.

During the next three months no one bothered me; I was left alone. The Special Branch seemed to have vanished out of my life. Except, of course, the restrictions on my freedom of movement or activities. These were still in force. I was a bound man, though the chains were invisible.

In December 1966, I went down to Kuala Lumpur to stay with my father-in-law in his Treacher Road house. When I went there I did not know another shock would come. Apparently all my movements were constantly observed, although I was unaware of the surveillance. Ten months had passed by since my release.

It was nearly lunch-time on 15 December. I was alone in the house with my son Zakaria. To my utter surprise suddenly a Chief Inspector of Police, accompanied by a Police Inspector, walked in. They gave me a letter by hand. It was another Order! They left five minutes later. Undoubtedly I had been watched, as they knew I was in the house. When I read the Order I was flabbergasted! Although the present restrictions I had to bear, but which I did not always observe strictly (as the Government well knew), were in force for a term of two years, and I still had another fourteen months to serve, this new Order extended my restrictions for a further two years—that is until February 1969. Why?

There could be only one reason I could think of that made any sense. Clearly this new Order was made to anticipate the contingency that I might possibly wish to become a candidate for the next General Elections, due in the first half of 1969 according to the Constitution, unless the Government called them earlier.

At first I refused to accept the Order. It required my signature in acknowledgement of its having been served. The Chief Inspector, however, told me that, irrespective of whether I accepted it or not, whether I signed it or not, the Order would be automatically legal. I still declined, so they left it on my table and walked out. Immediately I telephoned my friend and lawyer, Lal Devaser, in his office, but he said that regrettably there was nothing that could be done, except perhaps, make an appeal against the Order.

Then I telephoned the new Permanent Secretary of the Ministry of Home Affairs, Sheikh Abdullah, strongly protesting. A sharp exchange of words, but brief, as Sheikh Abdullah suggested I should visit him in his office next day.

God will forgive me if I gathered from our conversation that Sheikh Abdullah was not aware that the police had sent me the Order. But what he said confirmed my earlier deduction. He suggested the intention of the Order was not so much to restrict me in my movements, but rather to make sure that I would not take part in the 1969 Elections, by making speeches at the rallies held by the Opposition. All my earlier assurances that I was no longer interested in elections had been taken with a large pinch of salt by the Government, or rather by the police.

Still feeling a deep sense of injustice and quite dissatisfied with this conversation, I later telephoned the Minister's office, asking for an appointment with Tun Dr. Ismail. I was told I could call the following day. I spent an hour with Tun Dr. Ismail. During our talk I told him about nearly everything that had happened to me during my detention. He said very little, but he

listened to all I had to say. As a doctor and a man he was a good
listener, and had a reputation both for fair dealing and for being
outspoken. When I had run out of words, he said he would think
it over. We parted amicably. But I heard no more—the new Order
remained in force.

Two days later a Special Branch officer telephoned my father
at Gombak to find out where I was in Kuala Lumpur. He wanted
me to see the Head of Special Branch. My father told him I was
at the house in Treacher Road. He called on me there and asked
if I would come with him to Police Headquarters to talk with
the Head of Special Branch. Although he gave no reasons why, I
agreed to go.

When I met the Chief he referred to my talk with Tun Dr.
Ismail, concentrating on remarks I had made to the Minister that
I was writing and intended to publish a book about my detention.
I endorsed what he had just reported.

'If you persist in doing so,' he replied, 'there is no alternative
but to have you detained again.'

He did not refer, however, to my financial problems, which I
hoped to offset and resolve, as the proposed book had already
been accepted in advance by an agent for an American magazine
in Singapore. (It was, however, never published.) The Chief made
no comments on this information, and repeated his ultimatum
in the same words as before. With that, our meeting ended, and
I went back to Treacher Road.

Thinking it all over when I returned to Batu Maung, I concluded—quite reasonably, I thought—that it was clear the Government was still apprehensive about me. What else can one do with
an ex-Minister who is known to be as outspoken as Tun Dr.
Ismail himself? In their eyes, whatever I might say in all sincerity,
they would not accept in the same spirit. Obviously I was considered dangerous because my possible conduct was unpredictable.
I suppose they did not even believe that I was a reformed man,
because of my rediscovery of the great virtues of Islam. Somehow
or other I must be silenced and under the Internal Security Act
they had the power.

'And power has long arms,' I concluded. 'There is nothing I
can do but accept my present conditions in the true spirit of Islam,

which literally means submission to God. Time will surely prove me right.' So I surrendered myself to His mercy and continued my enforced retirement from the wider orbit of the world, leading a quiet life in Batu Maung again with the Koran and my daily exercise.

IV. BUSINESS VENTURE

So life drifted by for the next four months in Batu Maung. There was nothing left, surely, that they could wish me to endure. This time, I felt, I had really sailed into calm waters. But the daily routine was proving too much for me. I am an active man, I must do something. Writing was off the cards; I could not just walk or play golf all the time. I must earn some money in this year of grace 1967, Restriction Order or no!

I decided there was a possible future for me in the fields of mining or contracting. My idea was to engage in prospecting for ore, especially tin, either on my own or on behalf of others.

Although Special Branch had not bothered me during all this time, even though I was now and then breaking the restrictions by travelling to places on the mainland, or even to Kuala Lumpur, without asking prior permission, still I had better be careful before I ventured on such a promising plan. Experiences like mine arouse a sense of caution. So I rang Lal Devaser in April asking him to write on my behalf to the Ministry of Home Affairs to find out whether there could be any possible objection to my engaging in these forms of business. At the same time, to enable me to do so, would he also ask for the removal of my present restrictions.

Of course, I did not expect an immediate reply, so I went on counting the passing days and weeks. Perhaps they might add up to years, if things continued in this way. But I had decided that even if I was restricted, I was not going to act like a retired man. I was only fifty-three years old. So much yet to do!

Early in July I received a reply from Lal Devaser dated the 3rd, enclosing a copy of letter from the Ministry with the date, 30 June. It was an interesting letter in some ways, despite its official jargon. Addressed to my lawyer's firm, it stated:

Gentlemen

Encik Abdul Aziz bin Ishak

1. I am directed to refer to your letter KLD/MH/AZ/GF/Pt. 1/67 dated 12th April, 1967, on the above subject and to inform you that the Honourable Minister of Home Affairs holds the view that the present conditions imposed on Encik Abdul Aziz will not in any way impede his work or business if he is genuinely planning merely to be a miner or contractor.

2. Condition (1) merely applies to a change of his place of residence and does not in any way restrict his movements such as business tours outside Balik Pulau District. If, after having set up his business, he finds it more convenient or economical from the business point of view to move to a new District or State within Malaysia, this Ministry will certainly consider a request from him to change his place of residence. For this reason the Minister is not prepared to remove the conditions as requested.

3. The delay in reply to your letter is very much regretted.

As the 'above subject' I studied this letter with care and an occasional smile. They were still not sure of me, hence why the phrase 'genuinely planning'? Indeed I must still be a very devious, unreliable character from their point of view.

'Merely a miner or contractor'—hardly flattering to the many able men engaged in these activities. Hence the smile.

So I am allowed to take business tours outside the District under my present restrictions? If so, why had they not mentioned this flexibility a year before? I would have felt somewhat freer. It didn't matter now, I had been doing it anyway. Or was this a sly hint that they knew this and had overlooked my misbehaviour? Could be!

'Having set up his business.' Now, this was more promising, Obviously they would not hinder me in the elaborate procedure of registering a firm. There is a gesture of concession here. At least that's what it appears to say. I could move to another State or district, but note—'within Malaysia'.

So far, not too bad, but—with the Ministry of Home Affairs and its Special Branch arm there is always a 'but'—after I have gone through all those preliminary business procedures, perhaps in another State, 'the Ministry will certainly consider a request from him for permission, etc.' Still holding the sword over my head—that word 'consider'! Not just a simple 'Yes' or 'No'—that would be too much to expect. You should remember, Aziz, that Governments *never* like to commit themselves right away—they prefer to inch towards final approval.

Then the blow—and in such mildly-seeming words! 'For this reason the Minister is not prepared to remove the conditions as requested.' I would still be closely watched, even if from afar.

In effect, all that the Ministry had conceded was a blessing on my present rather-too-free travel, and an assurance that they would not stand in my way of going about establishing a firm. But if it meant moving from where I was, then approval would be considered. The whip-hand is still there—I am not off the leash. Rather disappointing, to say the least, and hardly softened by the confession of regret over their delay in replying. I was still a matter of concern to the Government—that was the fundamental point. They were telling me in their own special way—be careful!

Devaser had asked me to come and see him on this matter at a convenient time. So I went shortly afterwards, and asked him to initiate whatever procedure was necessary on my behalf to set up a firm to be known as Abdul Aziz Pty. Ltd. This took several months, but was finally accomplished, the firm being registered in Kuala Lumpur that year.

Simultaneously I started making contacts, exploring ways and means of raising capital, and at the same time deciding to move from Batu Maung in February 1968 and live in my father-in-law's house in Treacher Road next door to the Hotel Merlin. It turned out that this was a very sensible thing to do, as I could rent out my house at Batu Maung, and whenever it was free between tenancies I could use it as a holiday-home. The main asset was that this plan did work.

The Menteri Besar (Chief Minister) of Selangor, Datuk Harun Haji Idris, gave me a helping hand by giving me prospecting rights for tin ore over thirty-three acres of land in Selangor. That was a good start. I was beginning to feel quite my old self again. I had re- leased myself through my own efforts from some of my restrictions. But I knew they still applied, and, such is power, they could be reconsidered at any time. Outwardly I might appear free; actually

I was free on sufferance only.

With a rental income coming in, and a steady stream of contacts, raising capital here and there on the prospects ahead, travelling about to find land areas that might be worth investigating on contract for other investors, I was a comparatively happy and busy man.

My entry into the world of business lasted about two years. Then came an impasse. The area I prospected in Selangor turned out to be quite rich in tin. We had already spent $30,000/- to make this discovery. Then difficulties arose. Some of the land was occupied by people who owned it, but on most of the area there were squatters. We could mine the land if the owners and squatters would agree to move. None of them would budge. This being the main field of tin-recovery I had prospected, there was nothing I could do, otherwise it might cause some political embarrassment to Datuk Harun. So my business career petered out in 1970.

Meanwhile, I had been continuing with my writing. My second autobiography was half-completed, and I was noting down material for the book I planned about my detention. I carried on with both these activities in my spare time, even though there seemed to be no hope of their being published.

In December 1968, I suffered a grievous loss. My dear and greatly-beloved father, Ishak Ahmad, died at the age of eighty-two. He had been ailing with a heart condition for some years past, and at this time was a patient in the General Hospital in Kuala Lumpur and a widower, my gracious mother having died thirteen years before in 1955. He was a man of great humanity and true humility. A devoted Government servant, he had retired at fifty-five in 1941, having been Acting Director of Fisheries three times— in 1933, 1936 and, finally, 1939–41—while the British Directors were on leave.

In fact, the British authorities had such respect and regard for his virtue and integrity, that he was honoured with an M.B.E. in 1936, at that time a very high award for an Asian who was a civil servant.

Widely esteemed, he was born in 1886 in Trong, Perak, and had lived out his life as the simple, pious and industrious man he was. As a father, well, let me put it simply, we all loved and honoured him like a king. He was very strict with us, but always kind and fair.

My father had a great store of wisdom, gained from his knowledge of men, and a long memory which could bring out many stories of his times, always punctuated with pungent humour. Above all, he was a most devout Muslim. His faith in God knew no bounds.

His manner of death—quietly, calmly, rapidly—was typical of his whole life and character. One day in the hospital, soon after sharing a hearty joke with his physician, he went to the toilet. Then he came back, climbed on to his bed, folded his arms over his left breast as if in prayer, and with a smile on his face returned his spirit to the Hereafter, that world to which all of us must eventually go.

V. NEW REGIME

On Saturday 10 May 1969, the General Elections were held on schedule. I took no part whatever in them, as I had always said. Severe rioting broke out three days later—the fateful 13 May—immediately after the election results were known.

While I, like all loyal Malaysians, deplored this outbreak of violence, at least I had the quiet inner satisfaction of knowing that no one in the Government, from the Prime Minister down, could possibly say that I had any hand in that demoralizing tragedy. I was staying peacefully in my house in Treacher Road, and under curfew like everyone else. At no time did I see or encounter any violence. With one exception. On the second night a large wooden structure, to the rear of our house, burned down. It was the quarters of the Chinese staff employed by the Hotel Merlin.

Rumours were rife all over the city, and they grew and increased with repetition until they became nothing like the original version, whether that had any grain of truth or not. One of these concerned me, and, as usual, it sprang from the lively imaginations of some Malays. Word flew round that Aziz Ishak had been detained again! Special Branch had discovered a whole cache of ammunition and arms in his house in Treacher Road! It was false! For once Special Branch and I agreed!

After the 13 May riots began, the Prime Minister declared a State of Emergency. In fact, at this time of writing, there still is a State of Emergency, although most Malaysians seem to be unaware of this important fact.

About two weeks after this great calamity, various groups of people, all Malays, visited me. One group of two asked me for my reaction to the incident. I was suspicious of their visit, especially when they spoke adversely of the country's leadership

which they claimed required changing. Without hesitation I informed them that I had nothing to add to what they had said. The
leader of this group purported to be a businessman and left a
visiting card with me, inviting me to visit him at his office in Penang
if I felt I wanted to see him again. 'Perhaps we could do some
business together,' he said before he left.

Another group of three, all men of religion, from Province
Wellesley, came next. One of them I could remember, rather
vaguely, was a Haji who was an Imam in one of the mosques in the
suburbs. He was the spokesman. After a cautious attempt to review
my good work as a Minister of Agriculture among the farmers,
particularly the padi planters in the Province Wellesley area, he
asked me if it was my opinion that the present leadership would
bear the test of time and the circumstances then prevailing. I
immediately suspected a trap! This difficult and, to say the least,
embarrassing question caught me squarely on the horns of dilemma. Firstly, I could not make a reply that would indicate
condemnation of the leadership of the country, nor on the other
hand hypocritically praise the Government or even offer excuses
for the causes and effect of the 13 May catastrophe.

Suddenly I found inspiration in words of the Koran. A good
practising Muslim often chants after a prayer is over, reassuring
himself of his faith in Allah. Without much ado I quoted this
passage in a natural and confident manner:

> Say: O God!
> Lord of Power (and Rule)
> Thou givest Power
> To whom Thou pleasest.
> And Thou strippest off Power
> From whom Thou pleasest.
> Thou enduest with honour
> whom Thou pleasest.
> And Thou bringest low
> whom Thou pleasest.
> In Thy hand all is Good.
> Verily, over all things
> Thou hast power.

After this, the group left rather hastily, realizing that I would not commit myself to an opinion they were seeking.

I was living with my father-in-law in Treacher Road. One day in the first week of June, to my surprise, a Special Branch officer walked into my house. He was an Inspector, and he had another Order. I felt really angry. I refused to accept it. I asked his name. At first he would not say, but I insisted he should; so he told me. Then he tried to serve the Order again. I told him once more that I could not accept an Order for a still further extension of my present restricted conditions of release. He replied that whether I accepted it or not, the notice was to all intents and purposes delivered to me by word of mouth.

New regime or no, they were at me again! I could not understand why. I could think of no valid reason. It was all beyond me. I could only surrender myself to God.

Four years had passed since I was first released in February 1966. At that time I was told that I was no longer a security risk. Ever since the actions and surveillance of Special Branch had been exactly to the contrary. To them I was still a risk. They could not avoid letting me out, so they continued to do everything to make me feel they could not afford to let me alone.

'What will the next move be, if any?' I wondered. 'With that new Order they really have no need to do anything more—I am safe, they have made sure of that!'

After this Order, I moved again, in the third week of June, to my present home at No. 12 Gurney Drive, where I have lived ever since. It is quite a handy location in Kuala Lumpur. I was now paying more attention to my writing. Still under Restriction Orders, new ones, I did not notify my change of residence—I simply moved without asking permission. During my two business years 1968 to 1970, Special Branch left me alone, and this state of amnesty (shall I call it?) continued after I moved to Gurney Drive.

Of course, I read the papers daily, and journals too, keeping abreast of everything going on in Malaysia and the rest of the world. No journalist, if he truly has ink in his blood, can refrain from this daily habit. I did not have the same respect for Radio and T.V. Malaysia as I had for the printed word.

In September 1970 Tunku Abdul Rahman retired as Prime Minister, to be succeeded by his Deputy, Tun Abdul Razak.

'What was my reaction?' I began to think.

'There will be no fundamental change at all,' I concluded. 'Both men have always worked very closely together. Tun Razak is now Prime Minister and the Tunku has become Secretary-General of the Islamic Secretariat. The Government has granted him a house as his home and office in Kuala Lumpur. Where? In my old quarters, No. 1 Jalan Kenny, where I lived when I was Minister of Agriculture and Cooperatives. Destiny takes strange turns!'

How will it affect me in my present restrictions?

'I don't think there will be any difference,' I thought. 'Special Branch has still the same instructions, for the time being anyway. Maybe there will be a change, but since it has gone on now for four years, is it likely? Possibly, but I do not feel sure of that—not yet, anyhow. I will have to wait and see. Only time can tell. Wrong or right—which?'

In November 1970, my elder brother, Yusof, died in Singapore. Three-and-a-half years older than I, his had been the most distinguished career in our family, indeed he was outstanding among Malayans. When he died he held the highest office in Singapore, President of the Republic.

I went down to Singapore to attend the State Funeral in honour of his memory and his great services to the new nation. Behind his bier followed his only son, Imram. Just to the rear were my younger brothers, Ramley and Rahim and I, surrounded on either side and behind by the Prime Minister, Mr. Lee Kuan Yew, and all the Ministers in his Cabinet. They, and indeed the whole city, had come to pay a last tribute to a man highly esteemed by all. History will record that he was the first Yang di-Pertuan Negara (Head of State) when Singapore formed part of Malaysia for a brief two years, having previously served as Chairman of the Public Service Commission. When Singapore became a Republic, he was the natural choice to become the first President; he had earned this trust on his own merit.

But, I think that his true memorial, which will be evergreen, lies in another field. He was the first Malay to become a really eminent newspaperman, as he was the founder of *Utusan Melayu*, still the most influential Malay-language newspaper, and the core of the second most important newspaper-group in Malaysia. Formerly it had been published daily in both Kuala Lumpur and Singapore. I served my own years as a journalist mainly with *Utusan*. Yusof and members of my family held a considerable number of shares in this firm. In 1961 these had passed into public hands, being sold to UMNO.

Yusof had more of the characteristics of my father than Rahim or I. We younger brothers were occasionally hot-headed, certainly enthusiastic in whatever we did. Our older brother was tall, and the soul of courtesy, both in public and private. I have, of course, seen him rather worried many times, but he was always a man of self-control. Sufficient to say, his passing was a great loss not only to all his family, but to the people of both Singapore and Malaysia. As a Malay he was unique, since he played a very constructive role throughout his whole life in the building, not of one nation, but two. If I had inherited from my father his deep interest in fisheries, it was Yusof who was my exemplar as a journalist. My father was very proud of him, and so still am I. He never forgot a friend or a face. He had a number of disappointments in his life—the loss of the newspaper he founded was one—but he bore them bravely. I think it is true to say of him that he had opponents—what editor worthy of his salt has not?—but, to my knowledge, he never made an enemy.

In the next month, December, I had an interesting encounter. It was Christmas 1970 and I was on holiday in the Cameron Highlands with my brother Rahim, up from Singapore. By coincidence the new Prime Minister, Tun Abdul Razak, was also staying in the Highlands for two weeks' relaxation with golf, his favourite game.

I had not seen him since the elections in 1964, six years before, and it seemed very likely that sooner or later I must run into him on the golf course. After all, a golf links is invariably rather gregarious.

The inevitable happened. One bright morning I was playing with my brother-in-law, Dr. Johan Thambu. I had just finished putting on the fifth green when I saw Tun Razak and his party strolling towards the Club-house. He had finished his round. I felt I would like a drink, so did Dr. Johan. So we went into the Club-house lounge. As we entered Tun Razak and the members

of his party all stood up. Tun greeted me, 'Ah! Aziz. Come in.'
I thought he looked very much older than when I saw him last.
He shook hands with me, and introduced us both to his golfing
friends, all of whom I knew. One was Tunku Ariff Bendahara,
the timber tycoon of Pahang. We shook hands all round, exchanging greetings rather formally.

Then we separated, Tun and his party sitting at their own long
table, while Johan and I shared another nearby. After we had
finished our drinks, as we left to go on with our uncompleted
game, I raised my hand in greeting to Tun Razak, and he responded, smiling as we left.

Another of life's ironies, I thought. My old colleague was now
the Prime Minister. If I could have had a word with him alone,
would it have made any difference? That, of course, I could never
know.

VI. APPROACH

To my surprise, two weeks later a Special Branch officer came to see me in early January 1971. Actually I knew of him—he was a distant relation by marriage and came from Kedah. Despite this connexion, I felt caution creeping over me. What did he want? Conversation was general at first. Then he asked me whether I would be willing to rejoin UMNO, my former party, the core of the Alliance.

'No,' I replied, 'Why?'

Obviously there was something special behind this visit. Was I talking to an emissary, a chosen man? I decided to wait and kept silent. Then he said there was a new Government now, and so they might be willing to accept me back into the fold. So that was it. He was acting on higher orders, sounding me out.

'If I rejoin UMNO,' I thought 'then they will be really sure of me, and I will perhaps be given a position.'

'Does he not see the contradiction,' I wondered. 'It will look very odd indeed if a man known to be under restrictions is taken straight back into UMNO. It will certainly take some explaining to swing it.' I decided that the only course I could take now was to put the whole proposition squarely on the table on my own terms. Then I would know whether this strange offer was sincere or not.

'I will not,' I said, 'After all, they sacked me! I want to make this quite clear. I decline to be tied to any political party. First I must feel that I am truly free again. Then I can make my own decision as to what I may or may not wish to do politically. As I see it, there is no other way.'

He made no further comment, and left. I felt his visit had been a try-on, but it had failed. The fish did not take the bait. I had won a moral victory, and that was a very good feeling to

have. And the timing was wrong; I had far more important matters
on my mind, in my heart. For a long time I had been thinking
I should go on the pilgrimage to Mecca as soon as I was free.
Now the desire grew stronger, so I determined that I would take
part in the Haj that year.

When I went to make a booking, I met a setback. They would
not accept it. This dampened my ardour quickly, and for a while
I began to argue against myself. Then I shrugged off this feeling,
and became even more determined. I would get round obstacles
somehow, I simply had to go. I went to see Dr. Tan Chee Khoon,
who was at that time Secretary-General of the Gerakan Party,
and, as such, a member of the Opposition in Parliament. He was
famous for asking questions. He put down so many, either oral
or written, at each session that he had earned the nickname of
Mr. Opposition. Since my release I had never spoken with him.
But just some six months ago I had run into him briefly at the
Rest House in Kuala Trengganu, where I had stopped for lunch
on a trip back from Kota Bharu. Of course, we shook hands,
and had a short chat. Now I was going to see him because I
needed help. He is not a Muslim, but he is an able man who has
a way of getting things done by bringing up awkward questions.

When I told him about my predicament of being blocked whenever I tried to get a passage to Mecca, he immediately got on
the telephone to Sheikh Abdullah, Secretary General, Ministry of
Home Affairs. He said bluntly that if the public came to know that
I, a practising and devout Muslim, was being prevented from
performing the Haj, their reaction would be, to say the least,
highly unfavourable. Sheikh Abdullah promised to act on Dr.
Tan's suggestion without delay, and shortly afterwards there was a
definite change. The agents cleared my booking, confirmed my
trip, and accepted payment for my passage.

I went on the pilgrimage, performed all the many rituals and
duties laid down for proper and correct observance, and, like all
pilgrims I have met in my life, I can never forget the tremendous
spiritual uplift that comes from being there and visiting Mecca
and Medina during the pilgrimage, feeling a great and constant
elation of spirit.

When I returned from the Haj to my home in Gurney Drive

in Kuala Lumpur two Special Branch officers came to see me. It was 18 March 1971. I am afraid I did not act as a good Haji should. I slammed the door in their faces, telling them to go away. I thought they were going to serve me with another one of their Restriction Orders. But I was wrong. Through the louvres I could see them laughing and smiling. I could hear them calling out loudly and clearly that they were bringing good news for me. Carefully I opened the door, standing half-in and half-out, as I did not know what would happen. I was wary of news from Special Branch. After all, I had six years' experience of their ways.

They said they had come to serve a Notice releasing me from all obligations to comply with the conditions of previous Orders. I could not believe my ears. They handed me the Notice, and I took it. Allah be praised, it was true! With wet eyes I read:

NOTIFICATION OF RELEASE FROM CONDITIONS OF ORDER

'I AZIZ bin ISHAK do hereby certify that I have been informed this day that the conditions appertaining to the Extension of Restriction Order issued under section 8(1A) of the Internal Security Act, 1960, dated 22 FEB 69 have been withdrawn with effect from 21 FEB 71 and that I am released from all obligations to comply with the conditions of that Order after that date.

Date   18 February 1971   Signature ....

The above has been read over and explained in the English dialect to the above-named and his/her signature has been witnessed by me.'

I asked for a pen and put my signature on all the copies, retaining the original, which I still have. It is rather dog-eared now, having once been nearly burnt.

While doing so I pretended that I was not especially pleased by this sudden new change in my life. I thanked them very casually, and when they left, I closed the door with relief. Then I rushed into the kitchen to tell Wan Shamsiah, my wife, about this remarkably good news. She was busy cooking our midday meal and did not react very quickly. I realized she did not understand immediately what the implications of this Notice were. So I explained slowly to her that now I was really and truly a free man again, free to go anywhere—to Singapore, London, Japan, wherever I liked. Never again would I have to ask permission. She smiled happily, glad in heart for me, and, just like a woman, went on with her cooking. I noticed, however, that there seemed to be a little skip in her steps I had not seen for years.

Then I went up to my room to perform the midday prayer. At the end I thanked Allah with all my heart for having given me the strength, courage and patience to endure a long test of hardship, anxiety and humiliation, a period of trial and tribulation that had lasted for six long years. In my prayers I thanked Allah, too, for having allowed me to be treated in a way that was very much better than had been the lot of other people I knew. After their release some of them had to report daily to the Police Station where they lived; others reported weekly; and still others were under home-curfew, being forced to remain indoors during the hours of darkness. Alhamdullillah! Compared to them I had been much better off.

Next I hastened to telephone Devaser to inform him of my good news. He was very happy indeed, and congratulated me on the change in my fortunes. I also telephoned my brother-in-law, Wan Yahya, and a few of my very close friends, who had always been interested in my well-being during my detention and semi-confinement after release, and all of whom had helped me either financially or in various other ways.

At that moment I realized quite consciously, as if for the first time, that as long as I lived I would never be able to forget, nor could I ever repay the abiding trust and faith shown in me throughout these years of ignominy by all my children, and, above all, by my dear wife.

VII. FREE AT LAST?

NOT one single word of my final release appeared in the Press. Nothing was said over the air-waves. So my fellow-Malaysians did not know. Why this secrecy and silence?

When I was arrested I was front-page news. They made sure of that. Of course, their side of the story—not mine. I was in no position to answer back; I would not have been allowed to. Along with the news in the mass media, my political colleagues and all their auxiliaries down to the lowest ranks of power began a campaign of calumny, slander and vilification. In speeches all over the country, in cities and towns, villages and kampungs, they branded me as a villainous character, a double-dealer and, most particularly, a traitor. Now that I was finally free at last, they had nothing to say. In one sense I was alive, in another I was dead. Governments, unfortunately, can act in the most devious ways. It is regrettable but true that expediency is often the only immediate motive. This new tactic obviously was 'Forget him'.

This reversal of approach may seem surprising, but it was not so to me. While I was under detention, the Special Branch took every precaution to ensure that no news or photographs, no mention of my name or whereabouts, should be known to the public. Even I was sworn to observe this ban. As the reader knows, I broke that promise once, but that was an incident beyond my control.

When I was released, again the full barrage of the propaganda machine could be heard up and down the land. Even though I was freed (*sic*) they still made sure my name was blackened. They could not prove I was guilty, for the very simple reason there was nothing to prove, as I had done nothing. They let me go, but under such restrictions and in such a manner, that to most people I still appeared guilty. As the Government specialists in the art know, there is more than one way of killing a man—ruin his reputation, for instance.

After my very much publicized release, I received three separate Notices or Orders, extending the restrictions under which I would be allowed to live outside gaol. On each of these occasions, the Press was silent. Why?

The most likely reason is that they were not told. Or, if they were, it was off the record. Hence, they could not publish anything. After all, there is an Internal Security Act in force in Malaysia. So the silence on my official return to society was no surprise to me. Legally and technically, I was free, but publicly, no.

The Government had taken a very long time indeed to become finally convinced that everything I had asserted from the beginning was sincere—that I was not guilty, that I was no longer interested in politics, that my religious reform was genuine, springing from my own wish, and that I had carried out my word of honour in every way so as not to embarrass the Government publicly. Of course, I had caused them a lot of trouble behind the scenes, but none of these incidents or arguments or counter-actions ever came to light or became public general knowledge. They were internal. I am revealing them now for the first time.

Broadly speaking then, my return home from Mecca in March 1971 began a phase of new changes in my life. As I had fulfilled one of the major duties of a Muslim—one of the five pillars of Islam is to go on the Haj—I was now entitled by custom to be addressed by the honorific term, *Haji*. Instead of being merely *Encik* (the Malay equivalent of Mr.) I could be *Tuan Haji*. However, I did not, and still do not, use this form of address. I am not interested in titles—I never have been.

In the years before my detention I was approached on several occasions—three times by various States in Malaya/Malaysia and once by the Federal Government—seeking my consent to a title, but each time I declined politely.

My business venture had wound down completely, so, apart from writing, I had time to do anything that might be useful to the community. I had no intention of rusting away.

In June 1971 the Kuala Lumpur Book Club, a well-established private organization, dissolved itself to fit in with the changing times and progress of Malaysia by becoming the Selangor State Government Library. The Book Club members elected me as a member of the committee to represent them in the take-over discussions. So I became actively engaged in the library's work, especially on its rural extension project. Being a free man, with nothing much else to do, I could devote all my spare time to the service of the library. Of course, I worked in an honorary capacity; to me it was a labour of love. Today I am still an active member of the library board.

Around this time, I resumed my writing career, so fatefully interrupted by detention. Who was it who said, 'Out of evil comes good'? My detention had one good aspect—it was a new theme to write about. However, I was not ready to start as yet, as I had not finished an earlier manuscript—a further part of my autobiography. I had published an autobiography in Malay in 1959 under the title *The Frog Comes Out of the Coconut Shell*, a well-known Malay phrase, satirizing the narrow horizon of a kampung-dweller in colonial days.

The new work was designed to continue from there, covering completely the period of my active participation as a Cabinet Minister in the Alliance Government until my falling-out with my colleagues in February 1963. However, it did not work out quite the way I wanted. I kept on going away from and coming back to it for over two years. On completing the first draft, I took a hard look at what I had written, trying to be as objective as I could about my judgement. I decided the narrative had too much personal ego. It didn't sound right; it wasn't the me I knew. What finally made me decide to change my mind about going any further with the theme was the T.V. version of the 'Life and Times of Earl Mountbatten'.

Being part of history is one thing; making history revolve around oneself is quite another. So I shelved the idea, feeling it would be better for someone else to complete it. In fact, I dropped the whole project. But it is not abandoned, although I will not be its author. I approached the National Archives, donating all my private and public correspondence, speeches and photographs, which, I hope, are now safely in their vaults. When I handed over all these documents and files, they weighed 200 lbs. So these personal papers of mine are available to anyone who cares to conduct research on this period of Malaysian history. They tell what actually happened in my relations with my Cabinet colleagues, exactly as I recorded events and circumstances at the time.

I have nothing to hide from anyone. If I was guilty of the charges and recriminations levelled against me in 1963 when I left the Cabinet—one was that I was trying to project my own image in a quest for popularity with the people of Malaya—then the truth can be found in the mass of material I gave to the Archives.

While I was embroiled with this autobiography in 1971, I also began about the same time the story of my detention. Written in Malay, designed for Malay readers, I completed it within a year. But this book was to endure its own misadventures from 1972 onwards.

VIII. TOLL OF DEATH

ANOTHER sphere of activity engaged my attention in the latter part of that year. The Chief Minister of Selangor, Datuk Harun Haji Idris, invited me to become Deputy Chairman of the Board of Directors of a State Government Hostel for Malay Students and also the Selangor Foundation situated in Gurney Road opposite my present home. He himself was concurrently Chairman of the Selangor Foundation as well as the Hostel.

Students in this Hostel, some 300 in all, study to become doctors, scientists, engineers or general technicians. I accepted his invitation most readily, because it is the kind of constructive work I love. I felt that I could be of great help to them by emphasizing the need for personal discipline.

In fact, I welcomed the opportunity, as for the past fifteen years, like so many of my generation, I have noted with concern the general downward slide in standards among teenagers. Other days, other manners!

I am not the kind of person—there are too many—who wring their hands and moan about the generation gap, but do nothing about it. Who is to blame for the downhill slide does not matter; far better to try and do something about helping. That was, and is, my aim; my own experiences, good or ill, could help others, especially those who come from the rural areas and do not realise the pitfalls of city-life!

Early in 1973 another death occurred, that of my father-in-law, Wan Pawan Teh, who passed away in February in the Assunta Hospital, Petaling Jaya. Although he was a former Government officer like my father, no two Malays could be more unlike, yet their lives had strange parallels. Both died at well over eighty-two. Both were widowers; my father lost his wife in 1955, Wan Pawan Teh his in 1958. My father had retired quietly to our family home on a hill in Gombak, five miles from Kuala Lumpur. Wan Pawan Teh chose to live right in the busy heart of town, but he did not act like a retired man at all. Far from it, he became an acute man of business in buying and selling land. He had a successful career behind him, having been a member of the Malayan Civil Service—the 'Heaven-born' they were called in colonial times—and was very proud of the fact he could put M.C.S. after his name.

Wan Pawan Teh climbed the traditional ladder of the M.C.S. available to Malays in the British days—first as Cadet in a Land Office, then as Assistant District Officer, then up to the higher rungs of District Officer and Lay Magistrate. As a result, he was a man with very wide knowledge of the ins and outs of Government service.

After his retirement in 1940 he was frequently asked by Government to take on special posts on Boards or Commissions where his long experience could prove valuable, for example, Chairman of the Rent Assessment Board.

He was a good Muslim, but far more a man of the world than my father, and had always been very kind to me. He took a great interest in everything I did, although he often disagreed with my methods or ideas, always harking back to the good old days. But no man could have wished for a better father-in-law and he taught me much. To him I owe a great debt for his kindness, especially during my detention.

When Wan Pawan Teh died, he left a small fortune among the family. The sufferings we had undergone for six years past had, at long last, changed for the better. This is as it should be, in accordance with God's plan to change for either better or for worse. In my case, the better. Being a student of Islam, I was fully aware that it was strictly as He wishes it to be. Thus, during those years of suffering and hardship in my period of detention, I had endeavoured in faith to accept my circumstances with calmness and a stiff upper lip!

In the same year, three months after my wife's father died, I was highly intrigued to read in the newspapers the latest news of my former co-detainee, Ishak Haji Mohamed. At its convocation in June 1973, the University of Malaya had conferred on him the Honorary Degree of Doctor of Letters for his services to Malaysian literature. Although Ishak was in opposition to the Alliance Government politically, he had created a name for himself as a writer. An active journalist, he had written much fiction—novels and short stories, and continued to do so during the years after his release from detention. His works were highly popular among Malays. I had always thought of him as the Malay D.H. Lawrence.

What had happened to my other colleague in detention, Datuk Raja Hanifah, the man who exploded? After his release he continued to remain a faithful member of the Pan-Malayan Islamic Party (PMIP), which has now joined in coalition with the Alliance, especially in the States of Kelantan and Trengganu. Although born in Negeri Sembilan he was an M.P. for Kelantan, and so he was close to Datuk Mohamed Asri, the former Chief Minister of that State, who is now the Minister of Special Functions and Land Development. What could be more natural than that Datuk Raja Hanifah, for whom Islam always came first, should become what he is today—Deputy Chairman of the *Tabong Haji*, the Pilgrimage Board. No sinecure this post, as Malaysia, on a pro-rata population basis, has more pilgrims going to Mecca each year than from any other Muslim country!

Both my colleagues in detention had clearly risen in the world, despite the past tribulations we had shared. Both in a sense were clearly back in the fold—Datuk Raja politically and in Government service, and Ishak, no longer active as a politician, having resumed his old career, and gone on to newer heights, not only as a novelist but a feature-writer for *Utusan Melayu*. So to speak, they had cleared their names, had rehabilitated themselves in the good graces of those in power, unlike their colleague, Aziz Ishak, who was still out of favour.

Two months later Tun Dr. Ismail died in August 1973. I was playing golf that morning when I learned the news. I stopped my game immediately and drove straight home, and thence to Maxwell Road—now renamed in his honour—to console his widow, Toh Puan Norashikin.

The Government mourned the loss of Tun Dr. Ismail by according him a State Funeral with full honours. He was the first Malaysian to lie in state and be buried in the Dewan Pahlawan

(Hall of Heroes) at the Masjid Negara (National Mosque). Hundreds of thousands of Malaysians of all creeds and races filed silently under the great dome where his body lay to pay their last respects to a great Malaysian. I attended the State Funeral, as one of the members of the public, but found myself during the final burial rites seated among senior members of UMNO. Death—especially of a great man—brings all together in mutual sorrow. I prayed for him truly from my heart. I did not remember my detention then; I thought only of the man, my former colleague, his fairness, his outspokenness, and, above all, his dedication to duty in the service both of his fellow-man and of God.

IX. MY FAMILY

WHEN 1974 dawned I was already working steadily on this record of my detention, looking forward to the publication of another work, *From London to Jeddah*, due out in May, and had started on still another book, an authorized biography of Tunku Abdul Rahman.

The Tunku and I had agreed to work together, each one of us providing the facts, with myself writing his memoirs. We made this arrangement in August 1973, when he happened to be in Kuala Lumpur on one of his journeys home from Jeddah, his headquarters as Secretary-General of the Islamic Secretariat.

Promptly, the Tunku leaked our plan to the Press, announcing with his usual joviality that his life story was going to be written by Aziz Ishak, 'My former friend, and then an enemy, and now my very good friend again'. He officially retired from that post at the end of December 1973, but spent January editing and getting printed his Final Report on the Secretariat for the summit meeting of Islamic Heads of State in Lahore in February 1974. He did not attend that meeting himself, being officially retired, but he was already active on a new project, blessed in principle by the Islamic leaders, the establishment of an Islamic Development Bank. He and I talked often, either in Kuala Lumpur or Morib or Penang.

I did all my work at my home in Gurney Road, from which focal point my wife, Wan Shamsiah, keeps a maternal and grand-maternal eye on all our family. Most of my children I have already mentioned, but where are they now? And what are their interests?

My daughter, Rahmah, our eldest, who married Captain Mohamed Nizar, and was living in Singapore when I was arrested, is now teaching in the Convent in the Cameron Highlands, where her husband, retired from the Army, is Senior Assistant Manager of the Boh Tea Estates. They have two sons, Mohamed Razif, aged ten, and Rashidan, aged four.

Zakaria, my elder son, who is married and living in Kajang, near Kuala Lumpur, is managing a tin mine belonging to the Selangor State Government. He has a son, Mohamed Iswan, aged one.

Zubaidah, our second daughter—my wife and I have five— married Zainal Bachik, an Assistant Secretary in the Ministry of Defence. She herself is a producer for Television Malaysia. They live in Kuala Lumpur and have two sons, Zulkarnain, aged eight, and Zubin, aged four.

Zulkifli, my second son, is now working as a cashier in Malaysia Hall, London. Married and divorced, he lives at home with us whenever he is in Kuala Lumpur. We look after his only son, Hazim, aged four.

Zaharah, my middle daughter, married Captain Zainal Haji Thamby of the Royal Malaysian Field Reconnaissance Regiment. He is also retired from the Army now, and is Assistant Manager of the Boh Tea Estates in the Cameron Highlands. Zaharah is teaching at the Tanah Rata Convent. They have a son, Izal, aged six, and a daughter, Ida Zurina.

Raziah, our fourth daughter, was married in April 1974 to Baharom Hussein, an officer in the Ministry of Foreign Affairs. He is now at the Embassy in Manila. It was quite a wedding—just like old times! They have two children, a boy, Mohamed Zarul Nizam, aged two, and a baby daughter, Eliza.

Only Umi, our youngest daughter, is unmarried, but she is a very busy young lady indeed, being away in England at the University College, Buckingham, taking her degree in Law.

Wan Yahya, one of my brothers-in-law, is now the Parliamentary Draftsman, Malaysia, and another of my brothers-in-law on my father's side, Dr. Johan Thambu, is a gynaecologist in the Government Medical Services, working in Malacca.

On 3 May 1974 the whole family was delighted to pick up the daily newspaper and learn that Wan Suleiman, the brother-in-law whom I have mentioned as Solicitor-General, had made another step up the legal ladder. A few years ago he became Mr. Justice Wan Suleiman Pawan Teh, a Judge of the High Court, West Malaysia. The May news lifted him higher in the legal hierarchy, for he is now a Judge of the Federal Court, of which my friend, Mr. Justice Mohamed Suffian, is now Lord President.

My brother, Rahim, is still in Singapore and is now his country's Ambassador to Indonesia.

So, while I am busy with my own affairs, my wife, Wan Shamsiah, oversees the whole family. We have been married thirty-eight years now, and I never cease to admire her quiet confidence and optimism. She is a woman who can rise above any tribulation. Her natural shyness covers great strength of will. When I was detained she became a cooking-contractor, providing the food for weddings mostly from her own garden which she cultivated herself! A natural home-body, she keeps us all under control, not an easy task with our busy, widespread family of many interests, not to mention ten lively grandchildren!

Today my own life, apart from my writing, travels and business contacts, revolves around my two great loves—one spiritual, the other physical. Every morning and every evening I read and study the Koran. I do so continuously; when I finish, I start again. The Koran, which means so much to me, is a spiritual spiral linking all the days of my life.

The physical interest is golf. On a handicap of eighteen, I play six times a week at the Sentul Club with people of my own age, but some a few years younger—retired civil servants, industrialists, share-brokers, senior members of the professions. We are known as the morning golfers. I am devoted to the Sentul Club of which I first became a member in 1955. It might well be asked why I do not play at the posh club, the Royal Selangor. Well, I was a member once. That is, until I was arrested. Then they struck me off the register. One day I asked Tunku Abdul Rahman why they had done this. He said it was because I did not pay my subscription, I was a defaulter. As a reply it was rather naive. The Club knew I was in detention. With all the accumulation of wisdom among its many members it is surprising that someone did not remark, 'How can he pay his subscription, when he is a detainee? They are not allowed to receive or send any mail!' The real reason for my expulsion is, of course, that they believed I was a traitor to my King and Country, and as the Royal Selangor is under royal patronage, I was considered unsuitable.

No, give me Sentul any day. There at least the members, multiracial and tolerant, have a sense of humour, unlike the Royal Selangor. It never occurred to members there to have the wit to solve whatever dilemma I might have caused them by the sin of being detained to have simply written me down as an absent member.

X. MISADVENTURES OF
AN MS.

THIS book of mine is rather like me; it has had its own misadventures; in fact on its journey towards publication it has often been detained! Earlier I mentioned that I had completed the first version in Malay in mid-1972. It had taken me some effort to get around to actual writing even by that time—seven years after my detention, six after my release. The reasons why are now known; to say the least, I was preoccupied.

Knowing from a bitter experience of eleven years before what *could* happen to a book of mine, I had no wish to undergo the same frustrations again. When I was a Minister I had written and collated all my speeches and public statements relating to the first three years of my holding the portfolio of Agriculture and Co-operatives, 1955–9.

A fellow-journalist and an old friend, R.B. Ooi, who was formerly Editor of the *Singapore Standard* and later my own Press Officer, was arranging to have the book published. He sent the manuscript to the publishers soon after I resigned from the Cabinet in February 1963. I paid him $500 for the publication of 2000 copies, the balance to be settled after the book was out. He assured me it would appear on the bookstalls in about six months' time, that is, well before the General Elections in 1964. R.B. Ooi died suddenly in 1973 of a heart-attack. He was a fine journalist and a fearless editor, a man with a remarkable knowledge of many family histories in Malaya, including the skeletons! I am quite sure that what happened to my book was none of his doing. He was misled as much as I.

In those days the powers that be naturally did not want any book coming out that might be likely to boost my public image. How they managed to prevent it, I do not know. It is still a riddle unsolved, but strangely the publishers failed to keep their side

of the agreement. Whenever I tried to contact them they were
'not available'.

Two days after the elections were over in 1964, elections in
which I lost my seat, having stood as a candidate of the new
National Convention Party, which I founded, I had a sudden
surprise. I was living with my father-in-law in Treacher Road.
Getting up early in the morning to enjoy the fresh air, I found
bundles dumped on the verandah—the 2,000 copies of my book!
There they lay, brown-paper packs in the sunshine and shade,
with the title showing clearly, *No Compromise on Principles and
Policies*! Completing my manuscript is one task; the problem of
publication another. In my rather precarious situation in 1972,
it was obviously more tactful to try to get a publisher abroad
to produce the story of my detention. So, a year later, in June
1973, I decided to send it to Indonesia, as it was intended for
readers in Malay at that time.

I wrote to a fellow-journalist in Jakarta, asking if he would
kindly pass my manuscript to Mochtar Lubis, Editor of *Indonesia
Raya*. Journalists in South-East Asia, and indeed the world over,
have the greatest respect for Mochtar, who is without question
one of the great newspapermen of our day. I was hopeful that
he would help me find the answer to my problem.

He replied almost at once, saying he had received my manuscript
and would read it with the fullest consideration. Suddenly the
days seemed much brighter than I had known for some time!
So I awaited his decision anxiously; his good opinion would be
an asset indeed, especially if he should publish the work. Two
months later, I had still heard nothing further, but a happy encounter occurred. I was visiting Tunku Abdul Rahman at his
home in Kuala Lumpur, my own old house when a Minister.
It was two days after the funeral of Tun Dr. Ismail. I was out
in the garden, as the new Prime Minister, Tun Razak, had just
come to call on the Tunku. Who should walk down the drive
but my old friend, Frank Sullivan, whom I had not seen for ten
years. A journalist of wide experience round the world, Frank
came from Australia to Malaya in July 1948, arriving a month
after the Emergency began, as a correspondent for the *Sydney
Morning Herald*. He had been in Singapore in June, having worked

there previously from 1946 to 1948. Three months after coming to Kuala Lumpur, he resigned from his paper for personal reasons, and promptly became News Editor in the Department of Public Relations, Malaya.

He and I and A.S. Rajah, of the *Malaya Tribune*, became great friends, meeting together daily. The Coliseum Bar was our haunt. We were such constant comrades that we became known locally in Press circles as 'The Three Musketeers'. We thought alike, talked 'shop', a genial association that lasted three years, until Frank went down to Singapore again to join Radio Malaya as a Special News Editor. Over the next nine years our paths diverged, but every now and then we would run into each other. Our lives crossed again when he became Press Secretary to the Prime Minister's Department in 1958, a post he held for more than eight years. So he knew both the Tunku and Tun Razak very well. 'The Three Musketeers' were together again until 1961, when our friend A.S. Rajah unhappily died suddenly.

At this time, Frank had left Government service, and was running an art gallery, having been a founder-member and Honorary Secretary of the National Art Gallery for the previous fourteen years. He always called on the Tunku whenever he was in town.

Delighted to see each other once more, we strolled around in the sunshine catching up on óur scattered years, and recalling mostly 'dear old Rajah'. It was just like old times again—we were on each other's wave-length! I mentioned that I was going to write a book about the Tunku; the agreement had been made only an hour ago. 'Will you help me with the English version?' I asked, and he replied promptly, 'Of course, happy to do so.'

At that moment there was movement in the house. The Tunku and Tun Razak were coming out. We saw and heard them exchanging banter. The Tun got into his official limousine, greeting us as he drove by. Then we went in to talk with the Tunku.

I did not see Frank again for a few months, as I was travelling in Europe. On my return, feeling rather concerned about the lack of news from Jakarta, I decided to go over there to see Mochtar Lubis. That was in early December 1973.

When I met Mochtar he told me he would like to publish the book but there was no chance then of getting it done in Indonesia.

The difficulties were economic. He advised me not to publish it in Jakarta, as printing costs there were then twice as much as in Kuala Lumpur. Also, the shortage of paper was more acute in Indonesia than anywhere else. He was sorry, but it simply was not worthwhile to publish under such conditions. Not then anyway, the economics of publishing were against the idea. Perhaps these might improve but he doubted it would be soon. So that was that! There was no immediate chance of *Special Guest* coming out in Malay.

I returned to Kuala Lumpur with the manuscript, and started working at once on an English version. I did so because I still considered I must have the book published overseas; I did not want the possibility to occur again of its being nipped in the bud if I should bring it out in Malaysia.

On 6 January 1974, I met Frank in his gallery in the late afternoon, and gave him my manuscript. Naturally he thought the papers were the first parts of the projected biography of the Tunku. He said, 'I'll take them home with me and read them tonight.' At 11 p.m. the telephone rang in my home. It was Frank, and I could hear the tears in his voice, as he said: 'Oh, Aziz, I didn't know, I can't believe this happened. You, of all people, detained. I never knew, I don't understand how it could have happened. I'm so sorry.' Then his voice brightened, 'But it's a fine book, written from the heart, so absorbing.'

'It's not the manuscript you expected, is it?' I said. 'Will you still help me with the English version?'

'Of course,' he replied, 'very happy to do so.'

I put the telephone down, wondering about the oddities of life, and also feeling glad, very glad, twice over, not only because an old friend did not believe I could be guilty but also because we would be working together again, this time with our minds mutually directed to one objective—to get it published.

He told me when we next met that he was still baffled as to how it could possibly have happened that he knew nothing of my detention or release. There he was, working at the hub of Government until May 1966, and thinking all the time I was living quietly in retirement from politics down in Morib. He had concluded the only possible explanation was that he was away overseas when both events occurred, and no one had told him on either return. It was old news, and everyone took it for granted he knew. The odd, strange thing was he did not know.

I was happy with our reunion under these circumstances for other reasons. I knew Frank was a hard worker, having written hundreds of speeches in Malaysia on all subjects, always trying to make each one different and better. Moreover, he was as frank as his name, never afraid to say, 'I don't agree,' and give his reasons why. Like me, he believes deeply in truth. He often remarked, 'No matter how long it takes, the truth always comes out in the end.'

Quite frankly, although I have written full-length works in Malay, I do not think I would have dared to write a long book in English without his assistance. For me, the misadventures of this book were over.

So we began, and four months later, in early May 1974, the work was done and handed over to a publisher and to subsequent publishers.

I wrote in my Foreword that I was determined to tell the story of my detention, because I feel strongly that the people of Malaysia, at least, should know what happened to me when I was wrongly arrested and kept under restriction repeatedly for years after my release. Truth can indeed be stranger than fiction! As a true patriot I would never have believed it possible that such denials of freedom as I had undergone could ever have happened in Malaysia. And, what is more distressing, is the fact that others who have been detained, wrongly or rightly, may well have fared worse than I did!

On reflection, I wish to record here for the benefit of posterity that the first two governments of Tunku Abdul Rahman from 1955–63 of which I was a member, even at the initial stages were not truly interested in principle. That 'the leadership is always right' had been the guiding lines of the Alliance Government then. In fact, it governed more by expediency than by principle. Thus, truth, justice and sincerity were being bartered for their opposites.

Truth is often bitter to the taste of those who live in falsehood and profit by them.

Therefore, on reflection again, in the many years of my taking religion seriously, I can see that the future of our country, if it is to survive, must be based on the belief of the principles of Islam, where only through Islam can *truth, justice* and *sincerity* eradicate corruption and the abuse of power.

Injustice occurs all over the world. There is far too much suspicion abroad today, far too little true tolerance of our fellow-men. But truth and justice are one and the same in this; they find their own ways into the light. It is well for everyone who loves freedom to remember what Emile Zola wrote in his *J'Accuse*: 'If you shut up truth and bury it under the ground, it will but grow, and gather to itself such explosive power that the day it bursts through it will blow up everything in its way.'

He was writing about the famous Dreyfus Affair, 1894–1906, in which Zola's 'Open Letter' and the sustained campaign he carried on zealously in the Press of France, resulted in the clearance of the good name of Captain Alfred Dreyfus. Accused of being a traitor to his country, he was ultimately reinstated in the Army. Before Zola with his vast sense of truth began his attacks, Dreyfus had spent five years of a term of life imprisonment on Devil's Island.

I am no Zola, but my case is not unlike that of Dreyfus—on a minor scale. Whereas Dreyfus had a great writer of tremendous energy to come to the defence of his reputation, I as a former prisoner must publish my own defence. This I have endeavoured to do. The authorities in Malaysia responsible for my detention and restrictions have had their say, but there are always at least two sides to a story. This is mine, and it is true.

Now, at last, I can say my book is written.

INDEX